W9-BIL-425

EX LIBRIS

SOUTH ORANGE
PUBLIC LIBRARY

U. S. GRANT IN THE CITY

U. S. GRANT

and Other True Stories of

THE VIKING PRESS / NEW YORK

IN THE CITY

Jugglers and Pluggers, Swatters and Whores

DAVID FREEMAN

To Irving and Sara Freeman

309.1
Fr

Copyright © 1967, 1969, 1970, 1971 by David Freeman

All rights reserved

First published in 1971 by The Viking Press, Inc.
625 Madison Avenue, New York, N.Y. 10022

Published simultaneously in Canada by
The Macmillan Company of Canada Limited

SBN 670-74217-1

Library of Congress catalog card number: 77-148268

Printed in U.S.A.

The following page constitutes an extension of this
copyright page.

ACKNOWLEDGMENTS

"Lamont" and "Hector and Louise" originally appeared in different form in *New York*.

"Fat Bernie" and "The Fourteenth Street Swatter" originally appeared in different form in *The New Journal*, Yale University.

"Lydia the Tattooed Lady." Lyrics by E. Y. Harburg, music by Harold Arlen. Copyright © 1939, renewed 1966; Metro-Goldwyn-Mayer, Inc. Rights controlled by Leo Feist Inc. Used by permission.

"Chain of Fools." Lyrics: Don Covay. © Copyright 1967 by Pronto Music and 14th Hour Music, Inc., 1841 Broadway, New York, New York 10023. International Copyright secured. All rights reserved.

"Goodnight, Irene." Words & Music by Huddie Ledbetter & John A. Lomax. TRO—© Copyright 1936 & renewed 1964 Ludlow Music, Inc., New York, New York. Used by permission.

"Beat 'Em Cold." Copyright 1942 by S.U.S.A. Music, Ltd. Rights controlled by Arthur Farbstein, Inc. Used by permission.

"You Are My Sunshine." By Jimmie Davis and Charles Mitchell. Copyright 1940 by Peer International Corporation. Copyright Renewed by Peer International Corporation. Used by permission.

"Our Love." Words and music by James Scammo. Copyright 1939 by Waverly Music, Ltd. Used by permission.

"On A Clear Day (You Can See Forever)." Copyright © 1965 by Alan Jay Lerner and Burton Lane. Used by permission of Chappell & Co., Inc.

CONTENTS

FIRST . . .

There are more, of course—the people we almost know, loitering on the fringes, extras in their own movies. Occasionally one of them will pause long enough to become a celebrated lunatic, a public announcement of the city's famous brain damage: the rhythm band of dreamers and pretzel men who sing and dance their way down those cool streets mined with velvet and old jokes. There's a ten-year-old boy who spends all day on midtown subway platforms selling directions to people—a quarter will get you anywhere in Manhattan, fifty cents for the other boroughs. He makes $100 a week. There are private favorites, like the cop who walks serenely through Needle Park, past the pushers and the pushed, to ticket cars parked along 72nd Street. Or the news vendor on Broadway who got tired of giving directions and put up a sign: "Information 25¢" I saw the sign and asked him, "What is the secret of the universe?" Without missing a beat he told me it was fifty cents.

Here are a few who stopped to talk.

THE 14TH STREET SWATTER

In the early morning when the smog is soft and 14th Street belongs to cats, Elsie the 14th Street Swatter and dog lady stops for a moment to watch the sun come up over the 14th Street incinerator and listen to the Spanish Christmas carols playing in the subway station at Third Avenue. She smiles and plucks a paper flower from a trash basket and then moves on.

Christmas is the busy season for that sweet perennial scrawny lady with orange yarn hair and arms covered with tattoos, who spends her days leading her pack of dogs up and down the east end of 14th Street, foraging through the rubbish piles and garbage cans, saying Elsie is her only name, "Elsie, just Elsie . . . Elsie."

Her dogs—she has three regulars and occasionally one or two temporary strays—are called Elsie, Elsie, and Brownie. Why Brownie, a splendid if slightly ragged Irish setter, did not get in on the Elsies is a question that Elsie (the lady) does not answer. The canine Elsies are mongrels of the common street variety, and all three are as skinny as their mistress and usually a good deal dirtier.

Elsie and her dogs, like a French peasant and her hounds hunting for truffles, root through the side streets and doorways, foraging, but never taking anything. She just keeps turning over strange bits of cloth and half-broken objects, murmuring, "Now what the hell is this? What do we got here . . . ?" searching for some private and probably half-forgotten secret in the garbage cans.

Even if Elsie tends to leave trash alone, she does take bizarre liberties with passersby. She always carries a rolled-up newspaper under her arm which she uses as a club to swat strangers on the backside as they pass. The swat is no gentle tap but rather a sadistic smack, clearly meant to punish her victim. Happily for

those who travel 14th Street regularly, Elsie only swats occasionally. Usually her targets are so stunned at the idea of being
clobbered from behind that they respond in the best Manhattan
tradition, pretending it didn't happen and moving away from the
trouble as quickly as possible.

One victim of an Elsie swat, a ruddy-faced salesman in an
ill-fitting tweed car-coat, pushing a suitcase, on wheels, decorated
with a sleazy green wreath, did complain after Elsie whacked
him. The salesman turned and yelled at Elsie, who always keeps
walking as she swats, never breaking her stride.

"Hey you! You hit me?" No answer from Elsie, and the
salesman dragging his suitcase chases her and grabs her arm.

"Lego the arm," Elsie says softly.

"You hit me? Why'd you hit me?" Elsie says nothing; the
dogs relax on the pavement in front of the Orange Julius at 14th
and Third to watch impassively.

Elsie yells in a rough staccato, startling the salesman. "Hit
you? You crazy or something? Just lego the arm."

"Well somebody hit me. With a paper. You got a paper."

"You're crazy. Ask anybody." Elsie turns to the crowd be-
ginning to gather and to the patrons of the Orange Julius, who
stare indifferently, their faces distorted and elongated by the glass
walls.

"Did I hit him?" Elsie, screams to her audience. "Did I? Did
I? Did I?"

The salesman senses the incident getting out of control.
He mutters an ominous "Well somebody hit me," turns his suitcase sharply, and heads back down 14th Street. Elsie wakes up
Brownie and glides victoriously across the street to rummage
through the cardboard boxes in front of the United Cigar Store.

Elsie usually seems uncaring in her choice of victims; however, she occasionally seems to be reacting to injustices or to
some of the grossness that abounds in New York streets. One
morning about nine Elsie, caressing a box of trash in front of the
Blimpie's at 14th and First, looks up long enough to see two

middle-aged women in long black coats. One is carrying a shopping bag marked "Christmas greetings from John's Bargain Store," and the other is tugging at her ear. Both are jabbering loudly. As she passes Blimpie's, Ear-tugger accidentally steps on Brownie's paw, and Brownie gives an uncharacteristic yelp. The woman either doesn't hear or chooses to ignore the dog. Elsie drops the roll of slightly soiled brown wrapping paper she has been fingering and follows the women across 14th Street.

"He took a bum rap for her," from Shopping-bag.

"Yeah, I know," from Ear-tugger.

"On his own the dumb sonofabitch took a bum rap."

"Yeah."

"I'll kill the shmuck. He took a bum rap."

As Shopping-bag steps up on the east curb, Elsie pulls back a two-week-old rolled-up copy of the *Times* and swats each woman on the rear twice. Ear-tugger turns around sharply, ready for battle, but Elsie beats her to the punch with another quick swat, a rare frontal assault. Brownie barks again. Ear-tugger screams "muggers," and the two women disappear into the BMT stop at 14th and First. Elsie watches them go, smiling quietly, privately, and then marches away, forgetting about Blimpie's and the roll of wrapping paper.

Elsie always dresses the same way, just more or less of it, depending on the season. At the moment her year-round black woolen stockings are pulled down over her swollen ankles onto the tops of torn blue tennis shoes. Her red cloth skirt and blouse are dotted with dabs of brightly colored paint, and the pink moth-eaten cardigan sweater that is always with her is, for winter, draped elegantly across her back, its sleeves wrapped together in front. The khaki knapsack she carries for the swag she never collects is slung over her shoulder like a purse. Elsie wears glasses with round plastic frames that sit easily on a slender red nose that is usually runny and decorated with cold sores.

In warmer weather one can see Elsie's arms, and they are her outstanding feature. Each one is decorated with lush purple tattoos. On the left forearm there's a venomous snake coiled around a long dagger dripping three perfectly shaped drops of blood. Her right forearm has a large dog's head—a purple cocker spaniel, with a friendly-looking eye and its tongue hanging out. Below the dog there's a series of twisting, intertwined, almost psychedelic patterns of purple ribbons winding down onto the back of a hairy hand.

When Elsie wanders south of 14th Street into what's left of the hippie district, she pretends to ignore the crowds of kids on Second Avenue between Gems Spa and the Fillmore—but the kids rarely ignore her. A few of the hippies have seen the Marx Brothers in *At the Circus*, and when Elsie approaches they serenade her with a chorus from Groucho's famous song:

> "Lydia oh Lydia—
> say have you met Lydia,
> oh Lydia the tattooed lady . . .
> Lydia oh Lydia
> that encyclopedia
> Lydia the queen of tattoo."

Elsie enjoys the singing and the attention, and the hippies love to harmonize like a barber-shop quartet. For a while a few months ago it looked as if Elsie might set a new style among the hippies. They talked about getting tattoos for themselves, but the plan fell through when nobody could find a tattoo parlor. Now they seem content to sing occasionally "Lydia the Tattooed Lady" to Elsie and to wave after her as she roots her way up to 14th Street.

If some of the hippies have been watching Groucho, at least one of them has a more literary bent and has read E. E. Cummings. The boy, a tall, slender, effeminate Negro in Levi's and a denim vest that he wears over his cold bare chest, stops Elsie as she inspects two large cardboard barrels in front of Ratner's Dairy Restaurant, to give his version of Cummings' "my father moved through dooms of love." He lisps his poetic riff in a soft girlish voice:

> "sweet elsie moved through dunes of trash
> through stains of paint through halves of cloth
> deathing each morning into each night
> my elsie moved through dogs of fright."

Elsie looks at the boy warmly and touches his arm. He smiles, kisses her on the cheek, and offers a flower from his hat, but the gift frightens her, and she moves away. The boy blows her a kiss as Elsie heads south to Houston Street, and home.

The farthest west Elsie ever gets is Union Square. She works her way up Second Avenue, goes across 14th to Klein's, then back down the other side to Avenue C, down to Houston and across to the Bowery and home.

She rarely goes across the FDR Drive, usually stopping at the 14th Street incinerator. "I go where there's good stuff," she says. "But I stop down on the end by the big pipes, where 14th Street is in the sky."

Home for Elsie and her dogs is what's left of an old brick yard at the lower end of the Bowery, where there used to be a great many old-fashioned brick kilns—large red-brick domes with earthen floors and open hearths in which an earlier generation of craftsmen made the bricks and slabs of brownstone that built New York. The brick domes, like the artisans who worked them, are mostly gone now, but one—or most of one—remains, hidden behind a Bowery bar and flophouse, and Elsie calls it home.

The dome, which is about fifteen feet at its highest point and about twenty feet in diameter, is by New York apartment standards rather spacious. Elsie has run electricity from the hotel to her home with a Rube Goldberg patchwork of extension cords, zip cord, and black electrician's tape running down the hearth's chimney and into Elsie's quarters. The cord gives life to an old-fashioned floor lamp with a broken Tiffany shade that despite its damage would probably bring several hundred dollars in an up-town antique shop. Elsie also has a hot plate and a splendid-look-ing pink electric blanket with silk binding and dual controls, as well as a space heater. The blanket, Elsie's most valued possession —she's indifferent to the rest—is spread casually across an ob-scenely filthy mattress, which in turn rests on slabs of cardboard. The door to Elsie's oven is a tiny arched opening in the bricks— tiny in order to keep heat in, during the dome's more productive days. Now the opening is just the right size for the dogs, but Elsie has to crawl through on her knees. She keeps a pail of water near the hot plate; the dome, of course, has no running water. At night she covers the doorway with a wooden crate marked "Dried Norwegian Codfish: Heavily Salted." By day the crate is a bedside table.

Inside her dome in addition to her furniture Elsie has her "piles," mounds of carefully selected and arranged scraps of cloth, bits of plastic, and tinfoil and string—souvenirs from days when she did more than just pick through the rubbish. The order of the piles is very private and very distinct, and Elsie has obviously spent a lot of time keeping things straight. There are no apparent signs of Elsie's past life among her possessions, and the only dec-orations in the dome are two pictures torn from magazines, one of Marlon Brando in *The Wild One* and the other of Pope John XXIII celebrating mass at St. Peter's.

Elsie is unclear as to how long she has lived in the oven, but she cannot or will not recall living anywhere else. The dogs, Elsie, Elsie, and Brownie, live in the dome too. "Brownie, he sleeps with me all the time," Elsie says. "The other ones, Elsie and the other Elsie, just in the winter time. This time of year sometimes they sleep here; sometimes they don't."

Elsie seems to have worked out an arrangement with the flophouse that shields her from the prying eyes of the Bowery and allows for the use of the hotel's bathroom facilities. The hotel's manager, a gentleman not given to casual chats, seemed to think that the oven, like Elsie and her dogs, had always been there.

Elsie sometimes picks up spare change panhandling outside the Variety Photo Plays on Third Avenue near 14th Street. With her dogs asleep on the pavement, Elsie stands beneath the marquee and politely mumbles to passersby, soliciting "extra money." She keeps her rolled-up newspaper handy while she's panhandling, and when the mood is upon her Elsie swats her potential benefactors, black or white, rich or poor, whether or not they've given her money. Once in a while she goes into the Variety Photo Plays; in the morning admission is forty-five cents. On movie days, Elsie ties Elsie, Elsie, and Brownie to a parking meter in front of the theater and goes in to watch the double feature. She usually stays only an hour or so; then, concerned about her brood, or perhaps bored with Hollywood, she leaves and heads back to 14th Street.

For all her unusual habits and style, Elsie seems reasonably content with her life—or at least it hasn't occurred to her to question it. Perhaps the strangest thing about her is that, although she doesn't say it, one gets the impression that Elsie assumes everyone lives the way she does. Like all of us, she manages to find simple pleasures in her daily routine, and like all of us, she has her share of routine disappointments.

One of her greatest joys is playing with the small girls who skip rope on the sidewalks year round. The girls chant the same verses that girls have chanted for generations, adding only their Spanish accents. And Elsie loves to tie Elsie, Elsie, and Brownie to a fire hydrant or car bumper and join the chant:

> "Operator, operator give me number nine.
> Sorry, sorry, someone's on the line."

When they allow her, Elsie jumps, skirts flapping and tattooed arms waving, till she misses. She jumps as fast as she can, and the girls watch, squealing and giggling. Elsie, however, is a lousy loser, and when she misses, even if she's doing better than most of the ten-year-olds, she yells at the girls. "You twisted it. You screwed it up."

"No sir," is the indignant reply.

"You twisted it. You screwed it up on purpose."

"No sir. I didn't twist nothing. No sir."

The exchange goes on for a few minutes, till Elsie tires or the dogs wake up. But, before she moves on, Elsie takes a couple of free-wheeling swats at the girls and kicks fiercely at the jump rope, all of which serves to break up the game for the day.

Getting Elsie to talk about her past is almost as difficult as getting her to talk about the present. Like the true existential creature she is, talk of the future is out of the question. However, for the price of a roast-beef sandwich, a glass of beer, and a few raw-hamburger patties for Elsie, Elsie, and Brownie, she will open up a bit. It's hard to tell how much of her past is present fantasy and how much of it actually occurred; with Elsie it's impossible to know the truth. What is certain is that it's all very real to her.

She remembers growing up in Jersey City earlier in this century and as a teen-ager moving to New York—she can't say when, but she looks as if she's in her late forties. "One teacher, she always taught us about Indians. I learned about Indians from her," seems to be the most vivid memory of her childhood and formal education. Elsie worked for a time in the garment district, sewing dresses. "All day you worked there. It was hard, so I didn't go back." It appears that Elsie dropped out of the garment business in the late forties and has been living off the land ever since.

The tattoos are the result of a brief liaison with the owner of a tattoo parlor near the old Brooklyn Navy Yard. Told that the Brooklyn Navy Yard no longer existed, Elsie seemed surprised but not particularly affected by the news. She was most willing to talk of her most immediate problem, her ill treatment at the hands of area shopkeepers. She pulls on the stringy reddish-orange hair and stares at her beer. "They should just let us alone. We don't make trouble. We don't bother nobody. They won't let us at the stuff. If they don't want us at the stuff, why they put it on the street? If it's on the street, it's not their stuff any more."

Elsie has considered the question of ownership of "stuff"—street refuse—more deeply than any other issue, and she feels ill treated. Although she does not get emotional about the subject, it seems the closest she comes to caring about anything. "I don't go in the stores. . . . They shouldn't go in the street," is her pronouncement, and then she gets up abruptly to go outside and check on her dogs. She squats down next to Brownie, who is tied to a parking meter by the piece of clothesline he wears around his neck. Brownie is panting in the cold, and Elsie strokes his fur gently and scratches him fondly behind the ears, one of which is torn, and probably deaf. She mumbles something private and secret into Brownie's good ear, and stares across Third Avenue toward the Hudson Army and Navy Store. One of the Elsies reaches out her paw to shake hands, and then goes back to sleep.

Later, after a few more glasses of beer and a piece of apple pie, Elsie picks at a yellowed tooth and absent-mindedly fingers the tattoo on her left forearm. As she thinks, she begins to speak again in her rough-voiced staccato way, nothing for long periods, and then little bursts—as if she's hearing the words somewhere else and only repeating the message. Today she has Chiclets on her mind. It's unclear whether Chiclets is a man, or a dog long gone. She speaks of Chiclets, punctuating her reverie with jabs at her pie and sudden turns toward the door and her dogs.

"It was better when Chiclets was around," she begins. "With Chic there wasn't so much trouble with getting stuff . . . then we found all the best stuff . . . no trouble. Now they're all the time stopping me. Chiclets knew how to handle 'em all." She stops for a moment and roots through her knapsack, perhaps searching for some souvenir of Chiclets, which does not present itself. Asked if she expects Chiclets back, Elsie gets excited at the possibility and pushes a bony hand through her hair again. "He might," she blurts, "he might—you never know about Chiclets . . . it's a long time, but you never know . . . he might show. Then we'll start getting good stuff again. When Chiclets is around, you don't have to worry. Chickie can handle 'em all. They give me trouble all the time. 'Get out of here . . . get the hell away from that stuff . . .' But not Chic. They don't get so smart with Chickie. Chickie guards me. He guards all of us. Chiclets knows where the best stuff is. He knows where they hide all the good stuff. He knows Brownie and Elsie and Elsie and me and you. He knows it all. Chickie knows stuff that you and me never thought of. . . . Chickie knows where stuff is that you can't find even in dreams."

Each Saturday afternoon about two, Elsie shows up in front of the Evangelical Christian Church on 11th Street near Avenue B to hear the Bible-school chorus sing. The children, black, white, and Puerto Rican, gather on the church steps to serenade their neighborhood. Elsie usually watches and listens to the first few songs and then joins in when the teacher, a desperate-looking young woman about thirty, with mammoth breasts, adds an accordion accompaniment. As the boys in the chorus begin to giggle at the very real possibility of the teacher catching her bosoms in the folds of the accordion, Elsie smiles and joins the singing. She has a thin reedy contralto voice and absolutely no sense of pitch. But what she lacks in musicianship she more than makes up for with pleasure and joy in the music:

> "Jesus loves me, this I know
> For the Bible tells me so,
> Little ones to him belong,
> They are weak but he is strong."

Elsie looks forward to the singing all week, and after the half-hour concert, when the children have gone back to their lessons, she stares at the church door for a few minutes and then looks at the blue-and-red neon sign as it lights up, proclaiming "Jesus Saves." Elsie considers the possibility for a moment, and then steers Elsie, Elsie, and Brownie back toward 14th Street, looking for somebody to swat.

LAMONT

When Richard Nixon called for a program of black capitalism, he must have envisioned pulling platoons of bright young blacks out of the ghettos and plopping them down in the midst of America's romance with money. But the President has never heard of Lamont R., a Harlem native son and a black capitalist who makes $48,000 a year just "taking care of business." Cabinet officers will never invite Lamont to lunch, he's not listed in any phone book, and you won't find him in Dun and Bradstreet. There are no giggly miniskirted secretaries from Katharine Gibbs swirling around him, though he might like to meet a few, because at nineteen Lamont is one of New York's most successful pimps.

Although Lamont works in midtown Manhattan, he continues to live in Harlem, in a huge four-room second-story walk-up off 125th Street, near the Apollo Theatre. Lamont shares his apartment with Harriet, a handsome woman in her mid-thirties who is one of his employees as well as a principal recruiter of new talent. The apartment, like Lamont himself, is an adolescent fantasy of Turkish harem bedded down in French bordello.

Since Harriet's presence is more or less temporary, it is Lamont who runs the household. "You see all this furniture? I picked it all out myself—every stick. I didn't have no help. I'm the one says what goes here—furniture or people."

The living room looks like the Times Square Castro showroom: all the furniture seems to do something else—the couches turn into beds, the chairs become vibrators, the pictures on the walls have eyes that follow you about the room, and if you look at the rug in a certain light, the words "Let's do it" appear, woven into the fabric. Lamont has his initials, hammered into five-feet-high copper plates, hanging like trophies—an L on one wall and, opposite it, an R.

The *coup de théâtre*, however, is the bedroom. Never in

fifty years of movie-making has Hollywood come anywhere near Lamont's bedroom. In the middle of the room there's a gigantic bed, covered with fur rugs and satin pillows and mounted on a revolving stage. The obligatory overhead mirrors are there, along with lush plastic greenery that hangs from the ceiling, surrounding the bed in an African fantasy landscape. One wall is painted Day-Glo scarlet and the others are covered with larger-than-life photographic murals that could illustrate an Apollinaire novel. Of all the appointments in the bedroom, however, Lamont is proudest of his "sounds," a sound system (with speakers under the bed) that can envelop the room in jungle sounds, seashore noises, or stereophonic sighs. There is also a screen opposite the bed, on which Lamont shows pornographic movies and, when he can get them, old horror films.

Like some demonic character in an old Bowery Boys movie, Lamont also maintains an office of sorts. Operating out of a small luncheonette near Times Square, he sits in the back booth each evening and, like a cab dispatcher, takes phone calls, arranges assignations, and browbeats girls with cold feet or sagging spirits, or spars with the occasional bellboy or cabdriver who drops in looking to make a few extra dollars. Lamont has a fantasy, apparently inspired by Dick Tracy, of equipping each of his girls with a two-way wrist radio and of keeping a large map of Times Square, dotted with pins, so he can chart and keep track of each girl's progress and movements. Sid, the paunchy middle-aged owner of the lunch counter, keeps Lamont in rolls and Yoo-Hoo, the chocolate drink he constantly sips, as well as phone messages. Lamont keeps Sid in the action.

Lamont's been in business for himself for about a year and a half, and his evenings have now become quite routine. He shows up at the restaurant about nine-thirty each night. The girls report in ones and twos, starting about ten o'clock. Lamont gives each of them some cash, usually ten or fifteen dollars, "walking money," and sends them out into the streets with instructions not to come back until they've turned at least a hundred and fifty dollars' worth of tricks. Each girl has a small rented room or a cheap hotel room, depending on how long she's been with Lamont. The arrangements are made by Lamont when a girl first starts to work for him. Lamont's girls range in age from sixteen to forty.

When he first started, Lamont worked the streets himself, hustling business. Now his girls themselves are trained to solicit, and once they are dispatched Lamont sits back, sips his Yoo-Hoo, and waits for the money.

Lamont's staff is composed of one permanent assistant, Reggie, a boy of fifteen who runs errands and chauffeurs his boss's Cadillac—a silver Coupe de Ville with leopard-skin seats, four radio speakers, and an ice cooler for Yoo-Hoo. Reggie is paid about two hundred dollars a week, depending on how well Lamont does and how generous he's feeling. In any case, Reggie is one of the best-paid fifteen-year-olds in New York.

The rest of Lamont's staff is, of course, his girls, about twelve of them in all—with each girl working three or four nights a week. They're the ones who stand in Times Square doorways and in side alleys—the ones with the skinny legs and the spectacular wigs. Lamont has both black and white girls, and his pride at having an integrated company is his only apparent political act.

Most New York pimps recruit new talent in a time-honored manner, showing up any evening at the Criminal Courts Building after a Times Square roundup, and posting bond for any interesting-looking girls. Lamont, however, won't touch a strange girl. "You never know what you're getting that way—some of those chicks are really sick—you never know what you're getting. The jail's a good place to get girls if a dude's just starting out—you get a lot of quick talent there, it's like a cheap employment agency." Lamont wouldn't be caught dead at the "employment agency." For finding new talent, he depends on Harriet, the girls already working for him, and personal friends. Lamont runs a closed shop.

Lamont occasionally eyes a girl attached to another pimp. Sometimes he'll try to woo her away with promises of less work or more money; once he maneuvered another pimp's arrest and then moved in on the girl. If an independent girl stubbornly refuses to play, Lamont may be able to arrange for her to be busted, and then pay her bail if she'll join his stable. Recently Lamont kept after one girl, had her arrested and finally beaten by the police, until she agreed to work for him exclusively. While the girl was in the Women's House of Detention, in Greenwich Village, nursing her bruises and blackened eyes, sitting out her fifteen-day loitering sentence, Lamont had Reggie drive him downtown to the jail.

With the Cadillac parked on Greenwich Avenue, Reggie screams up at the red-brick walls and the barred window. "Hey, Darlene. Darlene, you up there?"

Darlene comes to the window and answers a wary "What?"

Lamont gets out of the car and stares up at the girl from behind his silvered motorcycle shades. He grins up at her. "That you?" he shouts.

"Yeah. It's me."

"How you doin'?"

"Okay."

"You want it again?"

"You gettin' me outta here?"

"You want it again?"

"No."

"Whose girl are you now?"

"Yours."

"That's cool."

Then Lamont gets back in the Cadillac and Reggie drives him back uptown.

Lamont doesn't have the black consciousness of most nineteen-year-old Harlem residents. For him, the color of the moment seems to be raspberry-lavender, with forest green running a tight second. The two colors are on the walls of his apartment, on a couch, and, in varying shades, on Lamont's trousers, of which he says he has forty custom-made pairs.

In a silver dish next to his bed, stacked neatly in a pyramid, is Lamont's collection of dildos—some wooden, hand-carved in Uruguay with pre-Columbian designs tooled into their surfaces, some plastic, stamped out by machines in Rahway, New Jersey, some black, some white, and some decorated with water-base paint that tends to run during heavy use. Lamont eyes them, flashes his Times Square smile, his teeth unzipping across his jaw, his eyes narrowing as he picks up an ivory number which vibrates with the power of two flashlight batteries and is sold over drugstore counters for "massage." Lamont runs his long fingers over the sloping surface and flicks on the switch at its base and then watches his little machine begin to shake. " 'Can you shimmy, can you shake, like your sister Kate,' " he says, toying with the device, and then he runs the dildo through the air like a child playing with a toy airplane. "We have some fine times with these, some fine, fine times," Lamont says, running the vibrator across the planes of his long loose jaw, massaging his neck and throat. He picks up another from the silver dish, a narrow banana-shaped one, made of hard rubber with a rawhide belt attached. "Watch this," he says as he swings the rawhide around his head in an indifferent mixture of sexual cowboy and Olympic hammer thrower. As the rawhide and dildo blur into a circle of potent energy above his head, he stands and fires across the room at his bedroom door. As the dildo bounces off the door, Lamont yells, "Hey. You in there? Hey."

Seconds later the door opens and Harriet, in a long, almost grandmotherly flannel nightgown, appears. Her deep brown skin is blotchy and her natural hair hangs limply. "Whatch you doin'?"

"C'mere, baby."

"Whatch you doin' throwin' that crap around?" Harriet moves the dildo with her toe, the nail painted gold and dotted with silver flecks.

"C'mere."

Rubbing sleep from her eyes and pushing hair from her face, she stumbles across the room, her feet caught up in the loop of rawhide in front of the door. "Whatch you want wakin' me up?"

"C'mon, baby, show how you do with this." Lamont flicks on his electric vibrating ivory drugstore dildo and hands it to Harriet.

"I'm sleeping!"

"Do it. Just do it."

Harriet takes the plastic device, flicks it off and then on again, stares at it, starts to hoist the hem of her nightgown, and then changes her mind. "You go round wakin' people up, I been workin' all motherfuckin' night. You wanta play with toys, you stick it up your own tushy." With that Harriet tosses the vibrator back to Lamont and retreats to her bedroom.

Occasionally, Lamont leaves his office to make the rounds. Reggie drives him over to Times Square and cruises around slowly while Lamont watches his girls in action, sometimes stopping to talk, checking on business or just shooting the breeze for a few minutes. The girls usually feel very flattered if Lamont comes to see them during the night. Frequently he will have Reggie park across the street from a girl so he can watch unobserved.

When he watches, Lamont looks for two things. "I don't mind if a chick goes for a cup of coffee or something—long as she keeps working. What I'm looking for is a girl who is hustling her tail off and then coming up with 'Oh, man, it was a bad night —I don't got no bread.' That's what I'm looking for. I play fair with them—but I don't want nobody knocking down on me."

Part of Lamont's success is due to his extraordinary control over the girls. Several recent newspaper articles, particularly in the *Times*, attributed a pimp's control of his stable to a quasi-mystic romantic sway over the girls. Lamont regards this as ridiculous. "They don't love me. Those chicks don't love nobody. They stick with me 'cause I take care of 'em. Everybody else is paying 'em fifty to sixty dollars a night—okay, so I'll pay 'em eighty. If a girl gets cut up, everybody else goes after the joker that did it. I get the girl a doctor. What does she care what happens to the guy with the knife? What she wants is to get herself taken care of. She's the one who's bleeding."

At six feet two inches and a hundred and ninety pounds, Lamont looks like the young men who play basketball all year round on black-top playgrounds, and in fact he moves as if he were driving in for a lay-up shot. Lamont did play basketball when he was younger. He says he used to have a reputation as a rough man under the boards, and no one doubts him. As a child, Lamont's hero was Goose Tatum, of the Harlem Globetrotters; now he follows the Knicks. Although he has never been to the Garden to see a game, he listens to the Knicks on the portable Sony radio that he always carries with him.

Had Lamont been born in Great Neck rather than on Lenox Avenue, he'd probably be a campus operator now at some place like Hofstra or Adelphi. He'd be the scourge of the sophomore class—the one who runs all the campus concessions from student laundry to newspaper distribution, with maybe a little side-dabbling in pot. He'd probably be a big man in some fraternity, quick with a firm handshake—the one everybody just knows "will go far in the business world." But Lamont has never heard of the Inter-Fraternity Council, and a term, to him, means the length of time a girl must spend in jail.

When he's not working, Lamont stays pretty close to Harlem. He goes to the Apollo frequently and likes to show up at high school and community dances. He spent a year in high school before dropping out at seventeen. He drifted around Harlem for about a year, in and out of the drug scene, in and out of petty crime. He's vague about how he got started in prostitution, but it appears to have been through a woman he knew who worked as a hooker on Broadway around Needle Park. She introduced Lamont to a few of her friends; Lamont provided all of them with the heroin that he always seemed to have, and soon he was managing their activities. Even the move from Needle Park downtown seems to have been casually made. One of the girls suggested it one night, and in accord with the laws of supply and demand Lamont found himself very rich very quickly.

Lamont now takes an understandable pleasure in strutting through Harlem dances in clothes that make most of the other young men gasp in wonder. With his Caddy out front, Lamont, in a pair of hundred-dollar alligator shoes and custom-cut raspberry-lavender trousers and alpaca sweater, bopping his way across a local gym or dance hall, creates a rumbling stir across the floor. The dancers, looking like off-the-rack parodies of Lamont, stop and stare in awe when they see him. Followed by Reggie, Lamont lopes easily across the room, eying the crowd. He stops for a moment, speaking to friends and bestowing status on whomever he greets.

Lamont at the dance is very like the king himself showing up for a medieval German court festival—the place is already rife with intrigue and power struggles—but when the Big Man arrives, the atmosphere becomes positively Byzantine, as the supplicants realign themselves in order to look good in front of Lamont.

Lamont stays only a short time, inspecting new girls, strutting for a moment or two, and handing out cash and pot in surprisingly large amounts to old friends or to anyone who has learned how to curry favor. He may invite a small group to go out with him for ribs and perhaps then to his apartment to turn on. To be invited to Lamont's apartment is an honor not handed out frequently and not accepted lightly.

Lamont pays no taxes on his income, so he has a great deal of money each week—and he spends it all. This is no easy task, as his tastes do not include French restaurants or the opera—or any of the New York establishments that make it easy to go through eight or nine hundred dollars every week.

Lamont would agree with at least one aspect of the *Times'* report on prostitution and pimps, and that's the importance of drugs. Most of the girls are into hard stuff, and Lamont is an important source—finding junk for them when they're broke and making sure they get a reasonably straight deal when they're buying. Lamont does not sell narcotics himself; however, he is well connected with the suppliers, and before he got into the far more lucrative and less dangerous business of flesh-peddling, he did push junk in Harlem. He turns on frequently, and occasionally takes a snort of heroin. He says he hasn't shot any of the hard stuff in two years. The girls are a different story; some of them have fifty- and sixty-dollar-a-day habits to support.

Lamont leaves Sid's early and tells Reggie to drive crosstown to the hotel where his friend and occasional mentor, a pimp named Finesse, lives. Lamont is clearly a solo operator, dependent on no one but himself, but he does occasionally seek counsel from Finesse, who is in his mid-fifties and who has made big money pimping since before Lamont was born. Lamont spent almost six months working on a trial-and-error system before Finesse would even talk with him and almost a year before he gave him any actual advice. Lamont is noncommittal about his actual parents, dismissing the issue with a shrug, and he would probably laugh at the notion of a father figure, but he does not deny that Finesse serves as a steadying influence as well as a source of information. "Old Finesse, he's always telling me to go slow, go easy, don't try to make all the bucks in one night. He's a okay old guy."

Finesse rarely goes into the street and seems to conduct all his business by telephone, by messenger, or by just watching out the window. During the day, he sits in his sixteenth-floor corner hotel suite, overlooking his street, watching his girls' activities. Finesse's girls, afraid of being mugged, work midtown streets only in the afternoons, retiring to bars after dark. The windows of Finesse's rooms are painted black, allowing no sun to violate his sanctuary. Narrow panes of one-way glass have been inserted in the corner windows, allowing Finesse complete privacy in surveying the street. Finesse lives alone, ministered to by Velvet, an epicene servant who favors processed hair and silver jump suits and who functions as Finesse's valet and factotum. Finesse himself seems to dress only in silk pajamas and smoking jacket. Finesse telling Lamont not to be greedy sounds like a Baptist preacher in rural Alabama. "You a greedy kid," he says. "You trying to make three hundred and fifty a day and it can't be done. It'll trip you up like all the rest."

"Shit, the day I make that kind of bread is the day I start robbing banks," is Lamont's reply.

Finesse is very conscious of the effect political administrations have on his business. He refers to all politicians by their first names only, not out of any apparent desire to give the impression that he's on a first-name basis with them, but more as if it were a code and he wants to make sure no one but Lamont knows what he is saying. "John is all right," Finesse says. "He gets enough trouble off the top with the city, he don't need to stir up any more. John, you leave him alone, he'll leave you alone."

Lamont nods his assent. "Dig," he says. "That's right."

"But Richard, now. Richard, he can be rough. Richard, he goes for the easy target, and—don't you forget it, boy—pimps and whores are the number one sitting duck up front easy target."

Lamont listens, nodding his head, repeating, "Dig, dig," almost to himself.

"Richard decides to pick a fight with John, you look out, he'll come down hard on you, me, and every international FBI whore you can find. You trust John as long as Richard got other stuff to make trouble over."

Lamont stretches his legs, twists his back, arching his neck. "Whatta we do?" he asks simply.

"We don't do nothing. We just don't get greedy and get on the wrong side of John. We just make our bucks and we don't make trouble. Long as we don't give John any grief on the street, then he won't give us any. And we keep an eye on Richard. Then everything's fine. Dig?"

"I dig."

"And you keep outta that street stuff. You stick to pimpin' and leave junk to the junkies."

"I know."

"Yeah, well I heard different."

"Whatch you think I am, some chile-ass popcorn kid trying to hustle a buck? I got a good thing, I don't need to mess it up with pushing junk. I know that."

"Good."

Velvet appears in the doorway and motions that Finesse is wanted on the telephone. Finesse scowls at Lamont, indicating the conversation is at an end. Lamont, a little riled at Finesse's suggestion that he has been fooling with narcotics, leaves the hotel and returns to the street, where Reggie and the Cadillac are waiting.

Although Lamont has a great deal of money, as well as the respect of most of his friends, pimping is not really his life's goal. What Lamont would really like is to be a pop singer and to play the Apollo. When he isn't listening to his portable Sony, Lamont frequently sings to himself and to the world in general, and he manages a fair imitation of Otis Redding doing "Dock of the Bay." But Lamont's love is saved for Aretha Franklin—that's his stuff. He reverently recalls the time Aretha played the Apollo and he watched all three shows, sitting down front, slapping his palm against his Sony, beating time. When Lamont recalls that night at the Apollo, his head rolls back and he rumbles into a near-perfect imitation of Aretha doing "Chain of Fools":

> *"Chaa, chaa, chaaen*
> *chaaaen a fooolz ..."*

The imitation is remarkable. Lamont catches her rhythms and her inflection perfectly, as well as a good deal of the passion. If pressed, Lamont will admit that his secret ambition isn't really to be a singer at all. What Lamont dreams of is making it with Aretha. "Sweet Aretha—she's fine all the time, baby—fine." It may be the only typically nineteen-year-old thing about him.

In addition to putting girls on the street, Lamont finds that to make it big in the hooking business one must spread the wealth around. He is hesitant to talk about payoffs, but a look at a week's take will show that a lot of extra money goes somewhere:

$150 x 5 girls:	750	nightly gross
80 x 5:	400	(girls' salaries)
15 x 5	75	(hotel and rooms)
	275	nightly profit
275 x 7:	1925	weekly gross
	200	(Reggie's salary)
	$1725	weekly profit

Something happens to about $800 of that money each week, and one thing is certain—it's not going to Uncle Sam. Lamont admits vaguely to "taking care of business." Although his girls are frequently picked up, Lamont himself has never been arrested on charges relating to prostitution. Lamont will not directly admit making payoffs to anyone, but he does carry a bundle of twenty-dollar bills in his pocket, and, if pressed, will acknowledge handing out a few "hats" each evening. (A "hat" is a twenty-dollar bribe, named in honor of former New York Police Commissioner William P. O'Brien's distinguished instruction to the force: "Nobody takes a bribe. Of course at Christmas if you happen to hold out your hat and somebody happens to put a little something in it, well, that's different.") A "hat" for today's force means a twenty-dollar bribe, and since the force rotates its Times Square assignments, Lamont finds himself carrying a lot of twenty-dollar bills. He fingers the twenties and mutters an ominous "Got to take care of the man—I'm getting mine, you're getting yours; well, the man's just naturally got to get his."

Lamont has practically no contact with the customers. He hears the girls complaining and talking about them, but they hold little interest for him. Lamont calls them all "smuks," a word that one takes to be something between sucker and schmuck. Lamont pronounces it with a long hissing sound.

Expansion holds little interest for Lamont. He doesn't care about branching out or enlarging—four or five girls working each night from a stable of ten or twelve is all he wants. He isn't interested in opening a house or even in booking call girls. Lamont just likes to sit in his back booth at Sid's with his Sony in the black leatherette case, sipping Yoo-Hoo and singing along with Aretha, waiting for the money to roll in.

HECTOR AND LOUISE

few years ago, when the moon was made of paper and a pleasant old man was President, Hector D. moved with his mother, his grandmother, and a platoon of assorted relatives from the slums of north San Juan to El Barrio in the slums of north Manhattan. None of the family spoke English and there were ten people in three rooms, but the rooms were big, the plumbing was inside, and the older ones took strength in little Hector, who was nine and had eyes the color of ripe olives and who seemed to learn English faster than he grew. On Hector's eleventh birthday the family moved to Simpson Street in the south Bronx and Hector moved to the streets, where along with more English he learned the ways of the subway and of airplane glue.

Two years ago Hector moved from Simpson Street to Avenue C on the Lower East Side, where he changed his ecstasy from glue to red wine in brown paper bags and then to heroin in glassine envelopes. Hector is still the only member of his family who can speak English and his eyes still look like olives, but green ones now, stuffed with red pimento. His relatives, or what's left of them, still live on Simpson Street, and Hector visits them occasionally. But Hector spends his days on the streets of the Lower East Side, where he and a friend named Louise share their nights in burnt-out buildings and support themselves by mugging their neighbors.

For a time, in the fifties, the streets that run east of Avenue A to the river and below Houston Street to the Brooklyn Bridge on New York's Lower East Side were almost a shrine, praised as the breeding ground of armies of doctors and lawyers, all of whom looked like Harry Golden. Praising the tenements of their youth ("Sure it was tough, but we had love and desire . . ."), Lower East Side alumni sounded like Nixon talking about his astronauts. Today the incipient Jewish judges are gone, and the hippies of a few years ago are mostly gone, departed for communes or the suburbs. The streets and the buildings, exhausted from generations of bright, aggressive youngsters followed by stoned hippies, look tired, as if they need a rest after sixty-five years of social ferment. Leo Gorcey and Huntz Hall are gone; the streets are lined with garbage now—human and automotive —and the people are mostly Puerto Rican. The billboards are in Spanish and in every store window a red sign screams, "How do you know you don't have V.D.? *¿Cómo sabe-Ud. que no tiene enfermedades venereas?*" The old-law tenements are crumbling, collapsing, burnt-out hulks. Their windows are covered with tin and plywood and their roofs are ripped away so that the sunlight floods into the upper stories like shrapnel.

When Hector and Louise aren't mugging their neighbors, they live in these buildings, moving easily from a deserted tenement on Avenue D to another south of Houston Street, near the Bowery. Always a few steps ahead of the wreckers or the Board of Health, they squat their way across the Lower East Side like spiders, spinning a chaotic web, leaving bits and pieces of themselves in each apartment. Sometimes they stay a month, sometimes only a few days. As they leave, Hector and Louise set fire to the building, and as their house and with it their past burns, they head for the next block.

Louise is seventeen, and although she has not been there in some time, she is, for the record, an eighth grader at J.H.S. 71 on Avenue B. Louise was born in Bedford-Stuyvesant, but grew up on Avenue C, where her grandmother still lives. Hector met her about a year ago in Tompkins Square Park, where they were both listening to a rhythm concert in the band shell. Louise was moving to the Afro-Latin sounds drummed on resonant empty fifty-five-gallon oil drums and Day-Glo-blue bongos. The six stoned Lower East Side drummers and the triangle man were deep in a private communal riff when Hector got up from a bench and began moving with her. They've been together ever since. Louise is slightly taller than Hector, heavier, and more muscular. Her skin is deep black and her short natural hair gives her a masculine look. Louise usually wears blue jeans cut off like pedal pushers and wedge-heeled sandals that expose her silver-trimmed toes. She has a bullet pendant that dangles from a raw-hide loop around her neck and settles gently between her breasts. The fingers of her right hand are decorated with Cracker Jack and midway claw-machine trophies: a red glass ruby, a skull and crossbones, and a narrow aluminum band that Louise says has the entire Lord's Prayer inscribed on it. C-H-I-C-O is tattooed on the knuckles of her left hand. These days Louise wears loose-fitting sleeveless blouses that expose her muscular biceps. The flowing blouse drapes easily over her swelling stomach and rests on the denim-covered haunches. Louise is five months pregnant.

Hector's jaw, pitted with clusters of bullet-hole acne marks, hangs open and occasionally dribbles a stream of spit across his delicate throat where the scars give way to bubbling, festering sores. At twenty-one, Hector is compact and wiry, and although his eyes are usually glazed and he often spends days on end in one of his apartments, picking at the scars on his arms and face, shooting up and nodding out, Hector is actually in better shape now, on heroin, than he was a year and a half ago when he was living on red wine. Hector, juiced out at nineteen, according to friends, was so filled with wine that his brain started going soft. Hector had been living on rotgut for about three months before he wandered over to the rhythm concert in Tompkins Square. Louise, who admits to having had her eye on him for some time before the concert, recalls his state easily, saying, 'He was so drunk that if you would cut him, his veins spurted Dago Red. Guys would go after him with a knife just to get a drink." Louise, who finds wine disgusting, changed all that when she introduced Hector to her very old friend, Snow White. Louise says she first took heroin when she was twelve. Unlike Hector, she seems able to take it in small doses and stop when she cares to. Hector says proudly, "Since I got on the horse, I didn't take a drink at all. Juice is bad for you, make you mushy. I'm all over that now."

Hector and Louise usually work whatever neighborhood they're living in. They knock over every old man on the block, every young man who follows Louise's swinging hips and pocketbook, and every young girl attracted by Hector's olive eyes. They rough up all of them, take whatever money is there, and then move on.

Their procedure is classically simple. Louise swings her purse and her hips and walks casually down the street. When someone starts following her, and someone always does, Louise wanders aimlessly toward Hector, who steps out of inner space and puts a knife to the man's throat. Hector tells him—only once—to keep his mouth shut. Louise, who has been standing there looking confused, starts to grin and steers her new friend into the shadows or into an empty hallway to rifle his pockets and take his wallet. The whole thing takes two minutes and then Hector and Louise leave as suddenly as they appeared. Occasionally a victim screams and Hector covers the man's mouth to shut him up. If that doesn't help, Hector must make a choice: cut or run. If he cuts, he usually gets excited and cuts again. If he runs, Louise will laugh at him. Usually he cuts. Not to kill, but to silence. Hector doesn't know if he's killed anyone. He remembers cutting one old man pretty badly, but he doesn't know if the man died. "He bleeded a lot. Like anything—thass all I know."

When Louise has picked up a likely candidate and wandered into Hector's shadow, she stops, lets the man catch up, and smiles and lets him move in. On Avenue D, that means a few sweet words and then some action. The victim starts pushing Louise into the shadows, pawing and babbling what he thinks is smooth talk. She giggles and protests mildly. Then Hector moves in. If the man has been rough with her, Louise sometimes takes the opportunity to spit in his face or kick him in the crotch. If it's a

woman and she turns out not to have any money, Hector occasionally rapes her. Louise helps him by gagging the girl and holding her arms or spreading her legs. Like the cook who loved
Mother Courage, Hector usually takes his women standing up.
Often he threatens to rape the girl and then, instead of consum-
mating it, urinates on her while Louise laughs. Then they both
kick the girl a few times and run. If her clothes look good to
Louise, she takes them along, leaving the girl to wander Avenue D
bruised and naked.

Although Hector and Louise have no permanent home, they
have established a bit of middle-class comfort in their lives. Hector and Louise are car owners, or more precisely, truck owners.
Several months ago a dry cleaner on Avenue B left the ignition
key in his delivery truck. Hector jumped in, and he'd been driving the truck ever since. Hector has no driver's license and in fact
can barely drive, but he and Louise practiced, careening around
the streets until now they can both manage to maneuver the
truck, a Ford, without too much trouble. They hid it in a gar-
bage-covered lot on 6th Street until Louise produced three gal-
lons of blue house paint appropriated from a renewal project on
Avenue C, and the two of them painted their mobile home with
rollers and a whisk broom. When they can afford gas, Hector and
Louise joyride around the Lower East Side at night. When they
can't find an abandoned building, they sleep in the back of the
truck. With a can of red spray paint Hector has scrawled "*Quiere
me*" on the right fender.

It's not hard to throw away a car on the Lower East Side—
in fact it's hard not to. Park it, take off the license plates, and
twenty-four hours later it will be stripped, an engineless metal
shell, covered with children swarming like ants, jumping on the
roof, trying to cave it in. Like an executioner offering his victim a last cigarette, a car vulture on the Lower East Side will always slide a metal milk crate under the axle, so that the machine
doesn't fall to the pavement while it's being stripped of its wheels.

The fleecing is done by children and adults in search of spark plugs, hub caps, and the like for fun and profit. Hector and Louise have escalated the war in order to equip their panel truck. In need of windshield wipers, they found them on a delivery van on Avenue D. Since that first set of wiper blades, Hector has taken to stripping loose parts from any car he sees, abandoned or not, and attaching the trophies to his truck. The truck now has four aerials and a myriad of reflectors, mudflaps, and tail lights. Much of the time Hector is not sure what he'll do with the parts. It's hard to sell spare auto parts in his neighborhood, where they are in endless supply, parked by the curb, free for the taking.

Hector and Louise, restless and broke—Hector with heroin but no reason, Louise indifferent—follow an old man in a long gray topcoat east on Houston Street past "Yonah Schimmel's Knishes," toward First Avenue. Hector walks casually, almost bopping to amuse Louise, keeping plenty of distance from the old man. Louise watches Hector's eyes follow the man's progress.

"What you looking at, boy?"

"Thass dinner up there."

"That's a nickel bag, that's what that is. That's a nickel bag of Snow White."

"Thass what I mean. Dinner. *Comprende?*"

Hector, staring at the man's back, walks a little faster, his hand in his hip pocket. Louise tugs at her bullet pendant and quickens her step to keep up. She touches Hector's elbow as they gain on him.

"He looks pretty old."

"Sure."

"Maybe he's a police."

"Some old man is all."

"A police, like an old man."

"Maybe."

As they pass an alley near First Avenue, Hector moves up on the man's left. Louise steps to his right, slides her arm into his, and begins to pull him gently toward her. As he turns to Louise, smiling and starting to tell her "No, no, I'm not interested," Hector pushes him sharply into the alley. Louise changes her gentle grip to a yank and pulls him into the dark. Hector follows with his knife open, swearing. Louise drops the man's arm and puts a tight yoke grip around his neck as Hector holds the knife to his stomach and fumbles for his wallet. The man begins to gag for breath and flutter his free arm. Louise tells him to shut up and draws the yoke tighter. Hector presses the knife against the man's stomach, cutting the fabric of his coat. He turns the blade upward and in one sweep slices the buttons off the coat. Louise knocks his wire-rimmed glasses to the ground and smashes them as Hector pushes the old man backward, across two open garbage cans. Two five-dollar bills. Hector pockets the money along with some loose change and he and Louise run for Avenue D.

Louise leans heavily into a broken door near the end of a dark and private hallway at her current address. She pushes it open with her shoulder and looks for Hector. He is sitting next to a shaft of light that melts through a broken window overlooking 7th Street. Nodding in the corner, his knees drawn up tightly against his bare chest, his electric-blue net polo shirt wrapped like a tourniquet around his left arm, Hector looks but doesn't notice her. Hector stares at the dust in the light, then moves his arm carefully into it, watching the specks settle on his forearm. He stares curiously at the red hole just below his elbow. The sores on his shoulder drip white fluid down his arm underneath the shirt tourniquet, to blend with the heroin on the lips of the red crater he is carefully cultivating on his inner arm, to avoid needle marks. Hector is always very careful to insert his needle in exactly the same spot each time. Hector touches the opening, caressing its edges. He purses his lips silently. As Louise stares, a pair of roaches crawl over Hector's works on the floor next to him.

The bugs work their way across his needle on the way to the tin spoon, where they stop and stare at each other in the stoned safety of the spoon's bowl. Louise, carrying two cans of collard greens stolen from the shelves of the Pioneer Supermarket on Avenue A, stands in the doorway and smiles at him. "You want some food to eat? Greens?" She holds up her trophies and crosses to him so he can inspect the cans more closely. As she walks, her sandals sink into the carpet of roaches that covers the floor. Louise, amused at the sound, listens to her weight crush the brown shells. Halfway across the room she stops and turns her heels on the wooden floor, as if she were doing the Twist. She looks at Hector's eyes, lifting his lids to peer at the traces of burst veins. Hector mumbles in Spanish and smiles back at her. Louise tugs at his short black hair and says, giggling, "Man, are you stoned." She pokes through his pocket for matches. "I'll make some greens." In the kitchen, she fills a tin saucepan from a gallon jug of water and lights a small wood fire in the sink. She adds the greens to the water and rests the pan in the fire. As Louise's makeshift stove flares up, it heats the greens and broils a geyser of roaches and ants that burst up from the drain into the flames.

Hector, moving down Avenue C away from his current home on 2nd Street, turns suddenly and heads west, searching vaguely for Louise. Suffering from extreme morning sickness, Louise has awakened early and headed toward First Avenue, looking for a free clinic she has heard about. Hector can't remember for certain whether Louise has left this morning or the morning before. Up till now Hector has been casual about becoming a father, preferring to let Louise worry about it. Sometimes he claims not to know about the pregnancy, other times he seems pleased with it. When Hector gets to Avenue A he begins to get edgy—anything west of A is alien territory and Hector knows it. Alien to Hector, and the home of the Alien Nomads. But this morning none of the Nomads seem to be out. It's a little past eight a.m. and the street is empty. Hector, following a private signal, like a bloodhound, Louise's scent in his nostrils, turns suddenly and heads toward Tompkins Square. "She gone to the cleen-ik, the cleen-ik," is all he can say. He keeps repeating it as he scans the streets. Near A and 7th, Hector finds what he's looking for. At the south end of the park Louise is curled on a stone bench, a few feet from a group of old men playing cards and rasping to each other in Ukrainian. Louise is moaning softly, a dark wet stain is traced on her lap and her throat is heavily bruised. The skin on her legs is shredded, hanging loosely, and a pool of vomit, flecked with collard greens, is on the ground in front of her. A trickle of blood drips steadily from her nose down onto the bullet pendant. Sensing his presence, Louise looks up at Hector, stares dully at him, and says, "Nomads."

"They beat you up?"

She nods and says, "I don't think there's no more baby, honey."

Hector sits on the bench, in the crook of her knees, touches the wet stain on her crotch and then dabs at her nose with his sleeve. "You get to the cleen-ik?"

"A whole bunch of Nomads. Gang banged me. Over there on Sixth Street."

"Sixth Street, huh?"

"There's some good houses in there. I was looking at the buildings. A whole bunch got me."

"You wanna move there? Sixth Street?"

"No, I wanna go to the clinic. Go home, get the truck so I could go to the clinic."

"Okay. I get it." Hector touches his sleeve to her nose again, and walks past the card game. At Avenue B he stops for a moment to talk to a man who wants to buy some heroin. Hector tells him he doesn't have any and then heads east toward Avenue C, trying to remember where he lives.

SYLVIA THE HOOKER

Sweet Sylvia, her nineteen-year-old giggles and grins buried beneath pink powder, her face like a street map of the Bronx done in acne relief: the lines under her eyes cross walks on the Grand Concourse, the space between her grinning front teeth subway tracks on the El along Jerome Avenue. Sweet Sylvia, down from the Bronx, living in the Village and making a few cherubic dollars on the side. Sylvia stands on Sixth Avenue just below 8th Street, where a collapsing demolished Nedick's is giving way to Nathan's Famous and where the Hare Krishnas turn around for the trip back east. Sylvia leans against the Manufacturer's Bank, staring at the remnants of the Village's annual shlock art and flimsy craft show, her platinum curls precise loops of silver set perfectly in place, lacing her forehead; her thin lips coated in ice-clear Revlon Nouveau Peach. Sylvia, perfectly turned out in Bronx silver and Village spangles, ready for the prom or the big pep rally or the two or three evenings a week she spends on the corner of Sixth Avenue and 8th Street soliciting her neighbors and their visitors, "Hi! Wanna date, wanna have a good time?" If you do, and if Sylvia likes you—and she never likes more than one or two a night—and depending on just how much she likes you, the price is somewhere between five and fifteen bucks.

Sylvia asks only "easy-looking guys, nice boys," and then if they're nasty to her, she refuses anyway. She lives a block away from her post in a tiny studio apartment overlooking 8th Street that looks like a college dormitory room—walls plastered with magazine pictures, the Beatles, Marlon Brando, the Stones, Warren Beatty, Jane Fonda in a silver jumpsuit, and paper revolutionaries, Huey in his Sidney Greenstreet Chair, Peter Fonda, and Ché. A small, under-the-counter refrigerator full of yogurt and diet soda and a sink full of dirty dishes complete the set. In addition to "liking boys," Sylvia is quite taken with the movies and goes to at least one each day. Her day is equally divided among her favorite (and in fact only) pastimes: going to the movies—good ones, bad ones, foreign ones, domestic ones—just movies—looking at clothes in the shops and boutiques along 8th Street and around Sheridan Square, and meeting boys. The three activities have dominated her life since she lived in the Bronx. The pickings these days, however, in clothing shops, movies, and boys are more varied. "I'm really glad I moved to the city, there's a lot of good movies around, and my social life has really picked up," she says. "I go to a different movie every day, and I go out with a different boy every night. At home they never changed the movies and the boys were all lousy and they never had any money anyhow."

Sylvia began her career as a liberated lady of the street while she was living at home, commuting in from the Bronx. "My father, he was working the night shift on the subways, and he used to bring me in with him. He didn't want to, but I told him if he didn't, I'd come in myself, alone. So he took me with him. I told him I was visiting my girl friend Kimberly, which I was." Papa Sylvia, a lifetime employee of the Transit Authority, escorted his daughter as far as the 86th Street stop on the Lexington Avenue line, and then nervously let her ride downtown alone, fears of mugging and fantasies of sin colliding in his head. Sylvia got off at Cooper Square, but instead of heading east for St. Mark's Place, the Electric Circus, and Gems Spa like all the other kids in from the Bronx, she walked west to 8th Street, where, true to her word, she met with her girl friend. "It was just Kimmy my girl friend and me and sometimes this other girl, Doris, but not too much Doris. Me and Kimmy used to walk around, look in stores for boys and toys and stuff. Kimmy used to rip off a lot of stuff, but I was always too scared. She could rip off anything, Kimmy. Once I ripped off this comb from Azuma's on 8th Street, only I was so scared when we got out that I dumped it down the sewer and then ran home to Kimmy's and hid in the bathroom. But Kim could do it everywhere, even

in the Big Apple grocery store where they have guards and secret television cameras that watch you. Some boys gave us money
once one time and we took it. That was around last year about."

Sylvia leans against the green plywood of the future Nathan's Famous-in-the-Village, smoothing the damp locks of her
platinum hair, pushing up first on her tilting beehive, then on
her breasts, pointing them at passersby, like bullets waiting to be
fired. She swallows two drops of Binaca breath sweetener from
her pocket bottle and waits calmly for the Hare Krishnas to go
away.

"Kim had her own apartment already, so after we got the
money the first time from those boys, we tried it again. It was
Kim's idea first. We needed enough money to go see *I Am Cur-
ious Yellow*. It cost three-fifty. Each. So we asked these boys who
were sort of following us around Whalen's if they wanted a date.
We didn't do it too much after that, once when we wanted to
see *Midnight Cowboys* and once when Kimmy wanted to go to
the Fillmore East to see Sly and the Family Stone. Only when
we wanted some money. We still went out on dates, but we
didn't get money too much. Sometimes we borrowed money
from the guys, sometimes we didn't."

Sylvia recently lost her business partner to love, when Kim
moved in "with this guy from the East Village." But, if she lost
a colleague, she gained an apartment. Sylvia lives in Kim's quarters on 8th Street by herself now. She still visits her family in
the Bronx once or twice a week to keep her parents happy—
"They think I work in a boutique, and my mother thinks it's a
good idea for me to get out on my own. They come to visit
once in a while, but they don't stay too long."

Sylvia finished high school about a year ago and then tried
her hand, for a short time, at higher education, as a nonmatricu-
lated night student at the Bronx Community College, studying
Fundamentals of Composition and Introduction to Accounting.
Sylvia stayed only one semester before she took off for the Village. "It wasn't exactly what I expected, I thought there would

be more of a social life. I mean, I knew they weren't going to have a football team, but I thought there would be more of a social life. You know, dances and stuff and hayrides maybe, and I'd be meeting more boys. But it was at night and it was only in this big building in the Bronx, and that's not exactly college. It just felt like more of high school, only not as hard. Most of the boys were too old for me and they were practically all married and they had children and jobs and they were real old. They were having riots and stuff when I was going there. The Port-o-Ricans were screaming and closing it all down. It was real exciting like in *Getting Straight* starring Elliot Gould, only with Port-o-Ricans so you could get hurt."

Sylvia's customers are mostly the young men who, like herself, come to the Village in the evenings from the Bronx, Queens, and Staten Island. They come hoping to pick up liberal bohemian Village girls. For most of them, Sylvia, who does not represent the threat of a Times Square hooker, or the mysterious unobtainability of high-cost call girls, is just right. She looks a lot like the girls they are used to, nice clean Bronx or Queens girls, and the powder she wears to cover her pimples makes her look slightly exotic and even a trifle erotic, without hiding her pudgy, almost painful innocence. Sylvia is anything but threatening, and for Bronx-honed tastes, shaped by horror stories of venereal disease, LSD, and heroin in the Village, she's the proper blend of innocence and adventure.

Sylvia usually looks for just enough business to support herself—keep her in shiny clothes, pay for the yogurt and popcorn and diet soda she seems to live on, and keep her in movie tickets. She has no taste for narcotics or liquor, and although she occasionally talks about saving money for a trip to Grossinger's or the Concord for one of their singles weekends, she doesn't ever seem to care about having any more money than she actually needs at the moment. Sylvia may not take drugs, but Kim was very into pills—upsies and downsies and in-betweensies. Occasionally, while Kim was around, Sylvia tried Dexadrine as a combination diet-pep pill. But with Kim gone, Sylvia no longer bothers with Dexadrine, and the bottles of brightly colored capsules that Kim left on the bureau and in the cabinets now sit out on the table as decoration. Sylvia went to a lot of movies with Kim, but she goes to even more now that her days are solitary. She always sits in the front row. "I like to be where you can't see anything but the movie. If you're in the first row and you look straight ahead you can only see the movie, no walls, no other people, no ushers. Just pure movie." Sylvia eats popcorn when the movies have it. "Sometimes they have those little cups of coffee, but not too much popcorn. It's getting hard to find." Sylvia frequently arrives after a movie has started and will just as often leave before it's over. "I go a lot because it's fun," she says. I sleep in late and always go to the noon one at the Waverly or somewhere. My favorite is Dun-stin Hoffman in *The Graduates*. That's more about what I thought college was like. Not like Bronx Community."

Sylvia stands in front of a dress shop on 8th Street, looking at a blue-spangled pants suit, with silver slippers. Chewing gum, she rolls her hip and balances her weight on her left side like a Hollywood whore, circa 1952. Carrying a bag of diet soda and yogurt from the Co-op market on Sixth Avenue, she stares at the clothes and taps her foot before she crosses the street to the 8th Street Cinema and the first movie of the day, *The Milky Way*. She sits in the dark, letting Buñuel and his views of Catholic dogma wash over her for about an hour, and then she stops looking at the picture to stare at the arm of light from the projectionist's booth. "I like to watch when they change the little windows," she says. "The movie comes out of one window for a while, then it comes out of the other. I like to watch for that." Sylvia walks out on Buñuel, and later announces her dissatisfaction with the movie. Usually when she leaves, she forgets the film immediately, but *The Milky Way* seems to be a particular disappointment. "I didn't like that one too much. I thought from the name of it, it was going to be about space or at least candy bars." Failing with Buñuel, Sylvia glances in the shoe-store window, and then at the glasses on display in the Eye Shop window; then she crosses 8th Street to walk the four flights up to her room. At home she washes her hair and resprays it with hair net, and watches part of Joan Crawford and Melvyn Douglas in *A Woman's Face* on Channel Five's Ladies' Day Matinee. Sylvia almost never goes to movies out of the neighborhood, and she doesn't usually watch them on TV. "Well, sometimes I do, like this one, or if I'm at my parents', but not too much when I'm here. When I'm here the movies on TV never seem big enough. In the regular movies they're all real big, the stars. Bigger than me, anyway. I like it that way. But sometimes TV's better than nothing. It's better than that *Milky Way*." She turns the TV volume up and assembles her hair-drying kit, spraying hot air across her head, talking above its din and above Joan and Melvyn's conversation. "I did this, making dates, I mean, more when Kimmy was around. We would both go out and it was easier, more fun with two. It's a little harder by myself and sometimes I don't feel like it. But it's not so bad. I'm finally meeting a lot of boys and that never happened before. Plus it's fun."

Sylvia paces Sixth Avenue, nervously looking for a date, dressed in a black Doctor Denton–style suit with a bib and a column of buttons up the front and a flap tucked under her crotch and pulled tight across her rump, with buttons all around. Her face is coated with the bright pink powder over a thin coat of Acnomel. Flushed with excitement at the prospect of "meeting new people," she stands a few steps from the subway stop, slightly to the right of two young girls asking for change, and calls to passersby—the young ones, or at least not the too old ones. Most of them pass by, smiling and ignoring her until a man about thirty wearing madras Bermuda shorts and argyle knee socks above his black leather shoes slows down, passes her, and then turns around at the corner. He pretends to have forgotten

something, snaps his fingers, and strolls back toward Sylvia, oozing calm and grinning charm.

"Hiya. Wanna date?" she says.

"What?" he answers, pretending to have just noticed her.
He tries to eye her body without seeming too obvious.

Sylvia pulls the bib top of her outfit tighter across her bust
and lowers her eyelids demurely, in an unconscious parody of
feminine subservience. "Wanna go on a date?" she repeats.

"Ahhh, I—"

Sylvia slips her arm into his, presses her ample bosom into
his short-sleeve Dacron wash-and-wear shirt, and says, "On a
date with me. Now. We could go up to my apartment."

"Yeah?" he says, jockeying for time and position, still trying to study her body.

"Sure."

"Well, how much is it? I mean—"

"Oh, it doesn't *cost* anything."

"It doesn't?"

"Well, you could maybe help me with the rent a little."

"Oh. Okay. How much is that?"

"Fifteen dollars would help."

With Sylvia's arm locked into his, a toothy grin spread over
his blotchy face, Sylvia and Bermuda shorts leave the corner for
Sylvia's flat.

"I stay with boys for a while if I like them," Sylvia says.
"Kimmy, she used to always get on a schedule. One hour and
then everybody off and out. It used to make me sick to waste
good boys like that, throwing them out. Sometimes I wish Kim
were still around, it's nice to have a friend, but double dates
were getting hard. I'm getting too old for that. It's easier by myself, too."

Sylvia walks along 8th Street, looking in windows, wonder-
ing what movie she should see. The pitch from one of the radi-

cal newspaper peddlers stops her. The seller, a frail young man about twenty, with sallow yellowish eyes and a scraggly, almost Oriental beard, carries a knapsack filled with papers printed on a flaky tissue paper. "National Liberation Front newspapers, direct from Hanoi, National Liberation Front newspapers, direct from Hanoi . . ." His cry has a musical rhythm to it, and he has learned just how much volume is necessary to fill his corner but not drown out the lean young black men and women pushing the Black Panther paper. Sylvia is enchanted with the lilt and rhythm of his pitch. She stops to listen to him. "Hear the truth from Hanoi, National Liberation Front newspapers, direct from—"

"Selling any?" she says to him.

"Twenty-five cents. The truth from Hanoi, in English."

"You selling stuff?"

Apparently used to girls who don't understand what he's doing, he makes his explanatory spiel quickly and smoothly, all the time keeping an eye on a trenchcoated crewcut, who is standing across the street casually observing him. "Read the N.L.F. point of view, direct from Hanoi, sister, only a quarter."

"Wanna date?"

Even though he ignores her overture, perhaps the privacy of their conversation, or maybe the way he says "sister," moves Sylvia to a rare political act. She looks at him fervently, raises a clenched fist, and shouts almost into his face, "Right arm!"

The Hanoi newspaper man stops, the Black Panther stops: both look at Sylvia and then at each other. Sylvia beams, and the Panther says to the Hanoi man, "Whatch she say, man?" Hanoi just stares at her, and the Panther asks again, "Hey gal, whatch you just say?" But before Sylvia can explain herself the crewcut begins to cross 8th Street and both newsboys move down Sixth Avenue quickly. As they leave, Sylvia lifts her fist again, repeating her slogan. "Right arm!" she calls after them. "Hey," she calls. "Hey." Crewcut steps out of the traffic, stares at her for a moment trying to decide if she's important enough to bother with. She smiles at him seductively, and starts to ask if he wants a date, changes her mind, and ambles back up 8th Street toward the 8th Street Cinema, where she'll see the first hour of *Au Hasard Balthazar*.

Around the corner from Sylvia's Sixth Avenue corner, down Waverly Place near MacDougal Street, is the Hotel Earle, seven stories of dirty brick, home of "Dr. Feelgood's Happy Time" and other assorted pleasures, resident and transient. Sylvia recalls Kim's fascination with the Earle. "She used to always sing that song 'You can get anything you want at the good ole Earle Hotel.' She always wanted to go over there and hang around. That place is a real funny farm. Queers and freaks all over the place. The place is always burning down and there's police and I don't know, all kinds of crazy parties. You can't even tell for sure which ones are the boys. Kimmy always thought it was fun to go there, but if I go somewhere to meet boys, I wanna make sure he's a boy. One time I saw this girl's rear end sticking out a Hotel Earle window and across the street some boy with a binoculars was looking at it. A naked rear end right out the window."

With the seasonal influx of college students and young people into New York, and particularly into Greenwich Village, Sylvia is looking forward to an active summer. "It's really crowded here. Sometimes when I get tired of all the social life around here, I go home to my parents' house for a while, just to relax. The trouble is my mother feeds me so much food that whenever I go home I gain weight. I put it on around the hips." Sylvia presses her palms into her stomach and sucks in her breath. She stares at the little ridges of flesh that ripple up between her pudgy fingers, and pouts at the sight of the flesh. "I gotta really start to lose some weight. I'd like to just once lose all the weight I need to lose. I'd like to lose so much weight that there wouldn't be any weight left on me at all. Just a skeleton with bones and no weight. Practically disappear, especially in the hips, so then I could wear the new styles."

"My mother gave me the pills first. We kept it a secret from my father. He would have blew his stack if he ever found out, but two years ago, when I was in high school, my mother started me on it. She was afraid I'd get pregnant. But I wouldn't. Not then. In high school? It wouldn't never happen. Maybe if I had made homecoming court it might have, but that's the only way. I'm still glad she gave 'em to me. I gave 'em to my girl friends sometimes. So I'm glad my mother gave 'em to me. She also told me about not using deodorant with aluminum chlorate in it. It plugs up your pores."

Sylvia stands in front of the mirror in her apartment, applying clear lipstick to her mouth. She stretches her lips and pushes her front teeth together, trying to close the gap between them. "When I was a little girl I used to hate this space. It made me whistle when I talked, and I thought it was really hideous. It was Kimmy convinced me that it gave me character, so I don't mind so much any more. I still wish they were closer together. Kimmy has stunning teeth." Sylvia pushes the teeth together again and takes a plastic spoonful of Dutch apple yogurt. "The best thing about having more money than before is besides the movies whenever I want, I could finally buy the stuff from Fredrick's of Hollywood. When I was a little girl my mother used to get the catalogue in the mail and I read it and dreamed about it. When I was a little girl I wanted a sheer nylon black negligee from Fredrick's of Hollywood more than anything. I have some stuff now that's really good." Sylvia puts aside her yogurt, takes two quick impulsive drops of Binaca, opens a drawer, and holds up a black and white bra with zippers running down the front of each cup. She drops it without comment and picks up another, a red strapless, with little street signs on each side, *I Go* and *4-U*. "These are only part of what I have and I'm gonna get more even. My dates always love 'em. Sometimes I put two of 'em on at once, but only for special occasions."

Sylvia leaves the Art Theatre's showing of *The Damned* in the early evening, after the five-o'clock show. She gulps three fast drops of Binaca to cover the smell of popcorn, arranges her jacket so it falls open just outside her breasts, and walks west toward Sixth Avenue "That was a pretty good picture. It was pretty crazy, but I liked all the clothes. It was sort of the *Bonnie and Clyde* look. I like that, it's stunning." Sylvia looks at the crowds as she walks, trying to gauge the people, sensing the men. "My favorite movie of all time is still *The Graduates* starring Dun-stin Hoffman, but my other favorite was *The Boston Strangler* starring Tony Curtis, and my all-time unfavorite is that yesterday one, *Milky Way*." Sylvia stares up at the spring clouds over 8th Street and looks again at the people crowding the sidewalks. She sidesteps a steaming pile of bright brown dog excrement and says, "I hope it doesn't rain tonight, I really feel like going out tonight," then she considers *The Damned* again. "That one part, where the crazy guy did it to that little girl? Eeeccch! There are some real crazy guys, though. Sick in the head. Crazy in the ca-beza." Sylvia winds a finger in a little circle next to her ear and rolls her eyes to show how crazy the crazy guys are. "And I won't go out with any of them, not me, that's for sure."

Anxious to see Kim, Sylvia sits on her building's stoop, spooning strawberry Lacto yogurt delicately into her mouth. She fingers a fresh pimple blossoming on her jaw and scans 8th Street. Kim has promised to visit and Sylvia seems nervous waiting. Kim, in bell-bottom blue jeans, with chic bleach streaks and a man's white shirt tied in a bow above her navel, exposing a belt of pink belly, her fingers decorated with rings, gold hoops hanging from her ears, and a few faded flowers stuffed in her frizzy hair, the baby fat clinging to her eighteen-year-old's arms and face, comes loping into view down 8th Street from the East Side. A torrent of words about Carl, their apartment, his film-making activities, pills and pot and the pleasures of life in the East Village, and Kim sits down on the stoop. Sylvia, entranced, listens and makes plans for another visit, to stay overnight, to meet again, to go to movies. Although Kim's current home is no more than a twenty-minute walk away, both girls talk as if Kim now lived in another country.

"I have this job," Kim says. "I'm in this movie, it's already done. It was real fun. It was terrific."

"In a movie?" Sylvia asks, stunned at the prospect. "Will it be around here? Can we go see it and popcorn and everything?"

"It was all made in this apartment and in Tompkins Square. I didn't star in it or anything. I was just in it. Another girl and this boy were the stars. You could do it. All you need to do is know the guy and have big boobies."

"Yeah?"

"Sure. We even had this big fake orgy in the apartment, and then we all ran down to Tompkins Square. It was fantastic. All these great boys all over the place."

"Did you do dirty stuff?"

"No. They were all really nice. A lot of boys."

"Gee."

"Well, you have to take your clothes off. For the orgy. But you don't really *do* anything. In the movie."

"What if my mother saw it and my father? Oh wow. Were there a lot of boys there?"

"Tons. I didn't go out with any of them. But you could."

Sylvia takes another dose of Binaca and considers the movies. "I don't know if I could do it. I might get a job as a go-go dancer."

"Yeah? That's fantastic." Kim adjusts the string of love beads around her neck, toying with them like a rosary. "Do you have a date for tonight?"

"I'm going to get one later."

"Like we used to?" Kim giggles. "Over on that corner?"

"Yeah. Hey Kimmy, call me when there's going to be another movie to be in."

"Sure. Hey, I have to go now. I can't stay. I'm supposed to meet this guy."

"I might not want to be in it, I might just watch."

"Sure."

"Okay, see you, Kimmy."

Sylvia watches Kim run up 8th Street, headed toward Sheridan Square. Kim stops to talk for a moment to one of the Panthers selling newspapers, and then disappears into the crowd. Sylvia takes another drop of Binaca, pulls her sweater tight across her chest, arranges her jacket so that her breasts tilt upward and point straight out like two fleshy magnets, and then walks over to her corner to start looking for a date.

U. S. GRANT IN THE CITY

Ulysses S. Grant, nonstop historian and reporter of fragments from a longer story, smiles at the morning crowd in Washington Square as he twirls a piece of soiled and frayed clothesline next to his knee. A few coins collect on the ground, and he pushes his cowboy hat back, smoothes his lank brown hair, and says, "This here rope and me we come a long ways together, we worked the Chisholm Trail and the long drive to Kansas. Me and this rope, we got a lot of stories to tell." Then, as casually as he began, Ulysses gathers his lariat and his coins and moves across the square, whispering to the gossiping nannies and shouting at the heavily mustached young men lounging in front the N.Y.U. Law School.

Ulysses will spend his day singing to the fountain in Washington Square, then dancing his way down familiar streets, sometimes insisting he's the Ulysses S. Grant, other times content to be a Ulysses S. Grant. And when there's no audience to listen and be entertained, Ulysses will wave his fist like a dog barking at a garbage truck and spend his passion screaming at the brick tenements that lead south from the park to Prince Street and into Little Italy.

"General Grant's comments were unprintable," Ulysses mumbles in his best Old South accent into the ear of an Instamatic-around-the-neck, *Underground Gourmet*-in-the-pocket pair of tourists who have surfaced on Carmine Street.

"Can you tell me where the Blue Mill Restaurant is?" the man asks haltingly.

"It's by the Cherry Lane Off-Broadway Theatre," his wife adds.

Ulysses grips each of them by the wrist, forming a triangle of secret urgency, and chewing off each word, adds, "But the President pondered the agent's report . . ."

The woman, her voice dissolving at the edges, clutches her husband's sleeve. "It's on Commerce Street. On fifty Commerce Street."

". . . before decidin' it was a fine piece of cattle wrestlin' and saddle slappin'."

The man, willing to forgo his street instructions, makes a blundering attempt to snap an Instamatic record of his private glimpse of local color, his brush with New York danger, but Ulysses, apparently through with talk, turns on his heel and moves back toward Sixth Avenue, leaving his friends still lost and fumbling with their film.

Ulysses is tall, over six feet, and even though he's old by street standards—maybe thirty-seven or thirty-eight—he stands erect, his body lean and tight with only a slight spread around the stomach; but Ulysses' face is tired, pouchy, pale as his muscatel, and his eyes are as empty as yesterday's bottle. "Hey look," he says, as he spreads himself out under the ornate cast-iron archway at Sheridan Square to speak to a pair of elegantly groomed Christopher Street homosexuals. "Hey look, what can I tell you. I'm in the wind—with you it's hair, with me it's wine. When the world turns around, who knows then, huh? What goes around comes around, huh? You're good men, you hear your music, I hear mine. I'm in the wind, and I don't know how long, but the general's going all the way next time, and that'll be how I'll hear the song." The men stare, then titter and giggle. The others sitting in the square—that dusty playground for junkies, winos, and old ladies in print dresses—stare at Ulysses, who, sensing an audience, climbs onto a bench armrest and balances precariously above the crowd. He smooths his workman's pants, announces, "General Grant's comments were primarily directed to the young lady, Miss Kathleen Robinson-Rorimer, a wasp-waisted, large-breasted, slim-hipped little razorback whose skin tasted like chunks of broken porcelain dipped in honey and who was, in the teeth of stiff competition, the finest whore in

Baltimore, Maryland. The general's remarks were, as previously reported in the popular press, unprintable, unrepeatable, and, insofar as they regarded Miss Kathleen's anatomical hot spots, highly ungodly and unbefitting a man of the general's station and achievement. But the President did allow how Miss Kathleen was as fine a piece of saddle beef as any in the East, and that he was favorably disposed to doing a bit of cattle wrestling himself, once he had drunk his morning coffee—a dollop of cream—no sugar and thank you very much."

In the morning, Ulysses drifts from Sheridan Square to Sixth Avenue and 8th Street and across MacDougal, back to the park at Washington Square. "I put on twenty-dollar boots and a Stetson hat and then I go to town." He panhandles some, steals some, and mooches in restaurants, specializing in sidewalk cafés. He wears dime-store six guns strapped around his waist and he keeps his eyes and wine private.

As Ulysses declaims and runs through his routines and numbers, he sounds as if he's reading from some bawdy, slightly arcane, and lavishly scatological book of American history whose chapters have fallen out of sequence. He affects an air of taking time out from more important pursuits to read occasionally amusing passages aloud. All of it sounds culled from private but highly reliable sources, elusive but desperately important. The coins that collect at his feet always surprise him, as if guests in his own home had offered him a tip for his hospitality.

"There is," he says as he stands in the doorway of the Bagel, on Cornelia Street, staring into the tiny restaurant and speaking just loud enough for his voice to fill the room, "there is a commonplace need aborning in the land: we must reassess our predilection for the playing at cards, the shooting of craps, and the smoothing of stones. We must adhere to the ethical principles if not the theological conceits and daily practices of the Anabaptists and realign our pursuits in the direction of our collective interests and pursue the common good, however we might malign, define, or refine it." Ulysses winks at the young girl behind the counter and smiles benignly as she places an omelet in front of a man in a pin-striped suit who is making an effort to ignore Ulysses. As the man salts his omelet Ulysses stares at him and reaches out to touch his shoulder. When the man flinches Ulysses picks up his coffee and takes a long swallow. "I remember once," he says, pacing through the tiny restaurant, along the counter, turning occasionally to the tables crammed against the wall, "playing stud poker in El Paso, Texas, for eighty-four consecutive hours. Stud poker and draw and we didn't get up to pee—the bar boy just moved a brass spitoon around under the big round table covered in imported green felt, and we would take our relief one by one, counterclockwise, as we played out our hands. One Mr. Frank James, lover of Carlotta and brother to Jesse, and mastermind of the glossiest money-gathering organization this side of the Internal Revenue and the most fearsome operation in the West, won and lost over forty-five thousand dollars government money in that game. He walked up to the table with four hundred dollars on a Friday night, sat down, ordered himself eight bottles of bourbon and six of rye, cut the cards, and proceeded to play and to drink. He continued to do both, nonstop, except for an occasional platter of fried chicken provided by the management, till Tuesday sunrise, when first the bourbon gave out and then the rye. He drained the dregs of the last bottle of Jack Daniel's, looked down at his stake, counted up nine hundred and seventy dollars, reported himself on the soft side of a winning streak, and declared, 'Gentlemen, the dog is out the door, the game is at the finish, I thank you for your sportsmanship and your good company, but now I must sleep.' And then Mr. Frank James walked directly out of that saloon, through a crowd of kibitzers and hangers-on that stretched from the table to the door, and was not seen in El Paso again until he and his brothers, in successful pursuit of twenty-six thousand dollars, shot their way in and then out of the Bank of Texas, some sixteen months later."

Ulysses says he has not always lived in the Village, which he refers to as "the frontier," or as "Panhandle country." He says he's been "living in these parts since Billy Quantrill, who was dead at twenty-eight, and his boys rode outta here on their palominos and left me and Virg to clean up the neighborhood." Merchants and park-bench regulars along Bleecker Street and on lower Sixth Avenue recall Ulysses wandering their streets since the early fifties. Everyone who remembers him from those days seems to agree that he is not much different from what he was then. Although he has only a few possessions, he does keep a dog-eared clipping from the *Village Voice* that confirms his apparent agelessness. The clipping is a picture of Ulysses at the front of a cheering crowd, waving and grinning at John F. Kennedy, campaigning in Washington Square. Now he has longer hair, but the Ulysses in the picture has the same high brow and aquiline nose, pouting mouth, and narrow eyes that sneak out of his forehead. If the face in the picture is a little less florid, a little less wine-soaked, it has the same balloon-like tension as it does today, as if it were about to burst, or float away. Aside from the clipping and the toy guns, Ulysses owns a rosary with several beads missing, a broken transistor radio, and a Texaco Know Your Presidents color print of Chester Alan Arthur, all of which he has stashed on Minetta Lane near what was once the Fat Black Pussy Cat Coffee House and dope-trading post. Those items and his clothes, along with an endless chain of bottles of cheap wine, are Ulysses' estate.

In the afternoon Ulysses stops to cadge his lunch at the Bagel, or at O'John's sidewalk café. In the early evening he visits the Waverly Theatre, where he frequently has good luck panhandling and where, if a Western's playing and the manager's not around, a friendly usher will usually invite him in to watch for a few moments. By early afternoon when he has scraped together enough money for his first bottle of wine—he'll drink at least two each day and a third if he can scrounge the price—Ulysses heads for the city basketball courts on Sixth Avenue, just below West 4th Street, to patrol the action and stand guard. The courts are busy all day and every evening, year round. In the afternoon teen-age boys from the neighborhood play, loping casually around the court, showing off, and rarely playing a full game with the same team start and finish. Ulysses struts along the sidelines, offering advice. The boys make a fuss over him, occasionally buying him ice cream from the Good Humor vendor, trying to draw him out. Two of the boys, thirteen and giggly, stop playing when they see Ulysses and come over to talk.

"Hey Liss-ee, hey man, Do it, man. Tell some."

Ulysses moves between them and clings to their shoulders, his eyes still on the court and the game. "Morgan and me rode over the plains and across to Topeka in three days, hard ridin', my little friend—"

"Thass right. Tell it, man. Tell that jive."

"Day and night and we ate raw buffalo and never stopped to camp. But we got there, and on time. The buffalo were there then, in herds so big the stench would kill a snake. All gone now, from Topeka and from the great plain. The buffalo all in the wind."

"Hey Liss. Do it. Do it."

"Play while you're young, boys, and only get it up for a buck."

"Sing, man. Liss-ees, sing a song, man."

Ulysses grabs one of the smallest boys around the waist, lifts him off the ground, and, holding him like a duffel bag, rubs his knuckles across the boy's budding Afro. While the boy, who is about nine, squirms and giggles, Ulysses sings:

> "Oh I rode inta Tulsa
> feelin' kinda low,
> thought I'd pick me
> up some dough
> at the Ro-de-oo."

Ulysses drops the boy, swats him on the rump, and switches his attentions to a more lucrative-looking prospect on the sidewalk near the court. A neatly dressed, slightly lost-looking young man about twenty-five is watching Ulysses banter with the boys. Ulysses is on him in seconds, speaking secretly, urgently, his hand encircling the man's wrist. "Friend, my friend, the cattle in the field are on the loose, the rocks are flowing down the mountain. Gimme a dime, I'll sing all the time, gimme more and I'm out the door. Gimme a buck, I'm down on my luck, gimme five or you're not alive." Ulysses whispers the last phrase directly into the man's ear, snapping the words until the man begins to quiver; Ulysses bears down harder on his wrist. "Hey look, brother"—he softens his voice but tightens his grip—"I'm in the wind and I need my wine. I'm in the wind and it won't be long. With you it's your hand in your pants in the alone at night, I can see it in your eyes. With me it's wine all the time, I can feel it in my throat. Gimme a break, gimme a buck." The man is frozen, his wrist in pain, his head confused from the flood of Ulysses' words. He jams his free hand into his coat pocket and fishes out a fistful of change and presses the coins into Ulysses' waiting palm. Ulysses releases his grip, turns sharply, and spins away up Sixth Avenue, forgetting about basketball. The young man stares at him and, as he watches Ulysses merge with the traffic, realizes that he has not said a word and has been fleeced of whatever was in his pocket. He begins to flush red, looks around quickly to see if anyone is watching, then suddenly, impulsively, crosses the street to get as far away from the spot as he can.

In the evening Ulysses' teen-age friends are spectators, and the courts are filled with men who have played asphalt basketball all their lives and who play hard, fast, and very seriously. The afternoon boys stand respectfully on the side, cheering or waiting for a chance to hold a towel. Most of the evening players—men in their late twenties and early thirties, men with jobs and families—are ex–New York high-school players. They are men who once dreamed of the Globetrotters and the Knicks. They wear old tee shirts with things like "Boy's High" in stencil letters across the chest, and they bet big money they can't afford to lose, on themselves and their games. Ulysses, attracted by the passion and the enormous expenditure of energy, likes to move around the edge of the game shouting encouragement. The men usually ignore him until he gets in the way. In a fit of exuberance Ulysses will sometimes try to join the game, running into the action and stealing the ball—no easy trick when the ball is being propelled down the court by the captain of the 1957 Boys' High championship team, driving for two points that can win him several hundred dollars. When Ulysses gets the ball (more by surprise than skill), he lopes across the court in an insane parody of dribbling, screaming, "On the trail, out of jail, where the Chippewas ride—yahooooooo!" Boy's High stares at him, frozen, as one of the two white players on the court, a paunchy, balding, redheaded giant, about thirty, with a blue bandanna tied around his head and a sweat-drenched sleeveless undershirt clinging to the wiry hair that covers his body, comes charging down on Ulysses, his lips dribbling saliva, a wordless scream locked in his throat. Ulysses connects with redhead's eyes and flings the ball, roundhouse style, into his crotch. As the ball hits and the man doubles over, his voice returns, oozing out, an agonized groan. Ulysses yells "Ya-hooooooo!" again and begins galloping to the gate, slapping his leg, like a little boy playing cowboys and Indians. Several of the other players chase him out of the court, screaming, "Hey you muthafucka, you get your jiveass outta here, I kill you. . . ." As Ulysses gallops away, he scales a green park bench, going over the heads of two girls watching the game, bounding straight into Sixth Avenue, where a bus and several cars swerve out of their lanes to avoid him. As he disappears down Sixth, one of the afternoon boys calls after him, "Hey Liss-ees, hey man, whatch you do that for? Hey Liss-ees, hey man."

Ulysses says he can remember everywhere he's ever been, everything he's ever done, and everything that's ever happened to him. His version of his origins is his most frequently recurring story. He has been polishing it, altering it slightly, imperceptibly, for years. He rolls it out every time he senses he's losing a crowd's interest, or when he can't find energy for the unfamiliar. It is both his tour-de-force and crutch, and he has done it so often he almost chants it: "My mother came across the Western plain in a Conestoga wagon during the big push of fifty-nine. My father, he sailed around the Cape in a clipper ship filled with spices and farm tools, bound for California. He docked in the Frisco bay and vowed never to leave dry land again and signed up for the Pony Express, ridin' from Sacramento to Saint Joe. My mother was headin' west, while my father was ridin' east, and her wagon train got lost in the Sierras, on the eastern slope, huntin' for the northern gap. While they were lost up there, two miles straight up to God, in the thin air and white snow of the Sierra Maestras with nothin' to eat but the horses and each other, my father rode over the crest of that mountain, plowin' snow and haulin' the mail. That they should meet was preordained. My father gave food and directions to the train, but he scooped my mother off the shotgun seat of my grand-father-to-be's wagon, strapped her to the back of his pinto palomino pony, and kept on for Saint Joe. The train made it into Frisco three weeks later, but my mother never saw California. I was conceived in a mail sack on a pony's back while the folks were takin' their ease after avoidin' a volley of hostile Comanche arrows. I was born sometime thereafter, just west of Topeka, where I was carried, cradled in my mother's arms, through the swinging doors of the Alhambra Hotel, and I didn't walk out till morning, when I was nineteen, singin' my songs, and on my way."

Ulysses in nighttime moving down Bleecker Street toward Carmine, on his way to nowhere, singing his own song, entertaining anyone who cares to hear:

"Rode inta Tulsa
Drinkin' my wine,
Got me a woman,
Singin' all the time.

"When Mr. James was young and ridin' with Billy Q., they talked politics but moved on blood. He and Quantrill and some boys from down the street rode around the country lookin' for federal throats to slit. Jess's job was to lure bluecoats into quiet corners where Quantrill and the raiders would insert long rusty knives into their Yankee throats and pull till those blue uniforms were red. Jess was seventeen at the time and he did his lurin' in dresses and perfume. Jesse, all smoke and dark velvet, would stand soft and fleshy in dark doors and alleyways and wave to the soldiers. The young ones, Jesse's age, would always come to look. And when they walked into Jess's darkness the only enterin' and violatin' that got done was to the throats of those former federal troops. Although he was the father of two and the lover of many, Jess took to dresses and perfumes as easily as he took to guns. Among Jess's women was one Belle Starr. With a hatchet face and a lavender plume she rode into Wichita on a horse named Venus in the spring of eighteen-sixty-nine. She swore, she drank, and she hated the sight of mirrors. She and Jess met at the long oak bar of the Kansas Thunder Saloon and Pleasure Emporium. Jesse tipped his hat and raised his glass to her, but Belle just stared and spit past him dead center on the brass cuspidor before she returned the toast. Jess took off his hat and offered it to Belle, who gave him hers. They stood there two hours, toastin', spittin', and changing clothes: one drink, then one garment. Hat for hat, shoe for shoe, till Belle was wearin' Jess's breeches and Jess was decked out in Belle's black-fringe-over-lavender skirt. When they had both drunk away the better part of the afternoon, they walked away from that barroom arm in arm and rode out of Wichita, headin' west. Jesse never tired of playing dress-up, and he and Belle masqueraded their way in and out of banks and telegraph offices all over the West for the next six years till even they didn't know who was who and which was which. Before he arrived at the house on the hill to hang up that final picture, Jess had taught his son to change clothes with his daughter and the lion to lie down with the lamb. Belle was far away and Jesse was bearded and thirty-four, and they buried him at the foot of a coffee bean tree in a five-hundred-dollar coffin.

> "Rode outta Tulsa
> Feelin' mighty fine,
> Had me a woman's
> Better than wine."

His allegiance to the past reaffirmed, Ulysses mumbles the last words and rhymes of his private report and then, oozing songs and dances to cover his path and guard his secrets, he wanders back to Carmine Street to hunt for a sleeping place among the doors, the alleyways, and the airshafts.

When the wine is gone and Ulysses is nearing the two-bottle stupor that envelops him about eight o'clock and carries him through the evening, he goes to see his friend Dominic, free-lance plumber, Carmine Street building super, and, after a fashion, Ulysses' confidant. Dominic is a squat, solid-looking man who keeps a clean building on a street of dirty ones. A Sicilian from the hills outside Palermo, Dominic usually wears grease-stained green work pants and white sleeveless undershirts, and he almost always chews on a plastic-tipped cigar. Dominic makes a quiet living tending the toilets and the water pipes in a string of buildings around Mulberry Street. Dominic speaks harshly of Ulysses. "I never give dat bastid no money—he justa piss it away." Dominic has talked to Ulysses longer than anyone in the neighborhood, and he takes him seriously by just accepting him. "He's around, I give him food, sometimes he stay here in winter, in a empty." Although Dominic will no longer tolerate Ulysses' stories, he does seem glad to see him each evening. Dominic is the only person able to deal with Ulysses on terms other than Ulysses'.

Dominic looks up from the copper pipe he is sorting and stripping for the scrap dealer, to greet Ulysses. "Hey you. How you doin?" Dominic lets his pipe wrench rest next to his leg as he relaxes against a garbage can.

"Hey partner, can I tie my bronco at your stable? He's ridden long and hard and needs a night in the hay. There's hard ridin' tomorrow."

"Hey you, shut up that shit. Why you always talkin' that crazy stuff?" Dominic nervously switches his pipe wrench from hand to hand. "Madonn!" he mutters, in a vaguely threatening manner.

Chastened, Ulysses drops his shoulders and sits next to Dominic on the lid of another garbage can. "Hey, hey," he says more to himself than to Dominic. The two men never use each other's name. Dominic usually settles for "Hey you" or "Amico," and Ulysses says "partner" or "pal" or just "hey."

Ulysses takes a long hit from his bottle of wine, offers it to his friend, who wipes the bottle's mouth, starts to drain the nearly empty bottle, then thinks better of it and tells Ulysses to put away the booze.

In the winter, when Ulysses needs to sleep indoors, Dominic offers him squatter's privileges in an empty room. But Ulysses usually has to be coaxed into sleeping indoors, where he is uncomfortable and frequently talks to himself, waking and jumping up. For now, Dominic urges him to go down to the basement and sleep. "Take a rest—on the couch, in the cellar—it's okay."

"No, no couches, no mattress. I'll sleep with God, under the stars."

"You talk about God? Madonn! Take a rest."

"I can only sleep alone. Or with God."

"Dat's alone. The cellar." It's an old story, and Dominic has heard it so many times it has grown comfortable for him. "You startin' bug stuff again? I cleana dat cellar with my own hands. I keepa clean cellar. No bugs. Not good enough for you?"

Ulysses holds on to Dominic's shirt, almost as if he were about to make a speech. But his grip is unsure and Ulysses is quieter, more intense than he is on the street. He speaks directly to Dominic, without the benefit of a smokescreen of patter. "They swarm out at me, when I turn on the light," he whispers. "And when I turn it out. When I get up to piss, they swarm at me. I'll piss in the dark, and won't turn on the light."

"Yeah, you usa the toilet. You do number ones on the floor again, I make you lick it up with you tongue."

"They come out of the floor and the mattress. A few only. But if I fall asleep, a lot. Hundreds, thousands. The floor and the couch get all black like a rug and when I go to the toilet my feet crush their shells and their backs. They are on the floor like beads, broken." Ulysses, his body full of liquid, begins to sweat, and his hands shake. His face and back are wet, covered with salt and sweat. Dominic, who has heard the story before, and who knows what his part is, shakes himself free of Ulysses' grip and says, "Hey, dat's all right, you don't have to go down the cellar."

"The beads cover my feet and get between my toes. I feel them. They are in the couch, and they'll get me. Baby beads, and they love my neck and my body. They'll put bug eggs in my ears. I can't see them, but I can feel them there. It's too dark to see bugs, but I can see their bellies, silver bellies, flashing in the dark, after they leave their eggs in my ears. I can hear their bug screams in my ears."

"They's no bugs down there," Dominic tries to reassure him. "I spray down there, and put mouse traps. Break their backs, snap 'em in two. No mouses, no bugs."

"They're waiting for the toilets to get filled up. Then they're going to back up and all the poop and all the pee is going to flow out of the toilets and onto me. That's when the bugs come out."

"Hey, take a rest for a while on the couch and you feel better."

But Ulysses doesn't hear him. Through with Dominic and through with talk, his bottle empty, he moves away. Stepping sideways next to the buildings, sliding his palms flat against the rough brick, moving fast like rope from a spool, Ulysses staggers toward Sixth Avenue, twising his neck, slapping at his ears, trying to shake out the bugs.

THE WORLD'S GREATEST JUGGLER

Bonamo and Dots, out of work and dreaming of Vegas and Ed Sullivan, ready to settle for a traveling circus or a county fair, lift their black vinyl trunk onto the Chelsea Hotel's double bed and pop open the gold clasps. Bonamo pushes the trunk over the bright blue twill spread and smiles as Dots shivers at the scraping sound. She wipes a handful of toilet paper across the trunk's stenciled letters:

BONAMO
The World's
Greatest Juggler

and Dots

Bonamo lifts his rolled-satin performing costume, brushes the wrinkles and lint from its spangled sleeves and gold slacks. As the folds turn to creases and the lint falls to the floor he hands the costume on its monogrammed velvet-covered hanger to Dots. She moves down the long hall to the closet of their Chelsea suite, their home base, straightening the 1947 Hollywood modern furniture, making tiny domestic adjustments as she goes, to the three rooms she and Bonamo lease annually and live in only six months of each year.

Bonamo and Dots talking of the international big top, the five-figure week and six plates on a pole in the Garden as Bonamo rests his arms on satin pillows and stares at the skylight. Dots drops an immersion coil into the Papa mug she has filled with the Chelsea's hottest tap water and plugs in Bonamo's breakfast. "If it was me only," she says quietly, "I'd drink it right from the tap. You can get a good cup of coffee right from the tap, if you use regular instant, not freeze-dried. If the water's hot."

"Coffee from the tap is barbaric," is Bonamo's pronouncement, with only a touch of his cool, clipped German accent apparent. He raises his arms to inspect his bony pale fingers. Thin but not frail, strangely epicene, Bonamo's lean body might belong to a dancer or a long-distance runner. He concentrates on his fingers in silence.

"If the water is real hot it's okay, only this Chelsea water isn't so hot," Dots continues, almost to herself.

"In my country," Bonamo says to his fingers, "the water is always hot, not like here. In all of Europe, even the peasants know the coffee will not flow from the tap." Dots watches the water bubble around the metal coil as she dumps a spoonful of powder into the cup. She stirs the brown liquid into breakfast and carries it to Bonamo, who sits on the edge of the bed and cradles the cup in his palms, breathing in the fumes before he sucks the coffee. "No cream?" he asks.

"Pream. We only have Pream."

"I'll drink it this way." As the coffee warms him Bonamo stands, tensed like a pilot before a flight. "I'll tell you a story," he says suddenly, nervously. "It is all I ever wanted to be." He begins to speak, the faint clipped accent precise and measured. "All I ever cared for was juggling. Years ago, before the war, when the other children were playing soccer or tag, I would go into the forest near our house, or to the edge of it. I was very afraid of those woods, they were dark. Very thick, and the trees—pines mostly—were very tall. There were stories of wolves that lived in the pines. 'In the pines, in the pines, where the sun never shines' was what we used to sing about those woods. But still I would run a little way in, to a small clearing at the edge, and throw. I was of course not the Great Bonamo then. I was Bonamo the young. Bonamo the minor, at a clearing in the woods, throwing balls or apples or eggs. Not juggling at first. Just throwing and watching things fall. Studying the way the air affects them, watching what happens when you spin them. Not juggling, not yet. For then, just throwing and falling. Apples, stones, pine cones, branches, flowers. I'll tell you a story. My mother had hens. Not many—seven or perhaps eight. Beautiful white German hens, and my job was to deliver their eggs. Of course I had to try throwing them. Eggs are wonderful to juggle, so smooth. Such a perfect ellipse." Bonamo stops his story to hold an imaginary German egg between his thumb and forefinger, and stares at it. Perhaps remembering the German forest, he flicks it into the air, flattens his palm to catch it, and then bows his head to Dots, who watches the exercise. She claps her hands, giggles, and cries, "Bravo Bonamo. Hurray Bonamo! Hurray!"

"Eggs," Bonamo says, "move through air with an inherent, almost instinctive precision. That they become such clumsy things as chickens is a remarkable shame. And if you are a ten-year-old boy in Lübeck as I was, and you choose to juggle your mother's eggs, you must learn to catch them. I suffered for days before I got courage to throw the eggs. I would walk past the path to my little clearing in the woods with my mother's eggs and try to find courage—nerve—to throw. Each day, for a week, I stood at the forest's edge, each day I would take a single egg from the basket and hold it between my thumb and forefinger and consider it. To throw an egg and watch it fall. To learn how much wrist action is needed to place the egg in the other hand, to throw an egg and reach your hand out to stop its flight. When I did it the first time I felt shivers and needles in my back. To throw an egg and spear it and stop its flight took my breath. The step to juggling, throwing two, then several eggs at once, was easy, natural. I was so nervous, I never dropped an egg. Even today, when I am throwing on Sullivan—in front of eight million people—I am not so nervous as I was in Lübeck with the eggs. Today, when I am getting careless—and I do—I get a flashing picture of my mother's hens and those eggs, and then I get careful again. That was about nineteen-thirty-two or three. After I learned to throw the eggs, it was simple to be a juggler. After eggs I began to experiment with the juggling of burning torches."

Dots, sitting on the bed, her long legs crossed at the knee, strokes her throat and then Bonamo's silks, and chews the first section of a Mound's bar with great precision: biting halfway through, a clean incision, she consumes the chocolate and coconut in several rapid bites, leaving only a few shreds on her fingers, which she licks clean. Dots, whose real name is Dorthy Dotson, has been touring with Bonamo since 1948, when she first saw him perform at the town hall in Indianapolis. "I was in high school—in Loogootee—and I was visiting Indianapolis. We went to the circus, the Lorgan-Marar circus, the whole class, and I saw him in his tights do a double shower with five red balls. I hung around for another day to watch again. He wouldn't let me be his assistant for a long time. Finally he did." Dots, approaching forty, still looks remarkably like the teen-age girl in the photograph she always carries, the one now on the Chelsea's fake fireplace mantel. The photograph, taken at the old Frontier Hotel in Las Vegas in the early fifties, shows Bonamo, a little heavier and with a little more hair, balancing a cane on his nose. Just to his left and slightly to the rear, standing in a ballet dancer's second position, her full Loogootee high-school cheer-leader's breasts bulging behind a pink tutu, is the former Dorthy Dotson, the planes of her face a little softer, her blond hair a little fuller, her legs a little more muscular. Bonamo, his teeth perfectly matched and as bright as enameled billiard balls, stares straight ahead. Dots, slightly out of focus, her eyes in their perpetual cross, seems hypnotized by the cane on Bonamo's nose.

A farm girl from Loogootee, Dots grew up just ahead of television, and knew little more of jugglers than what she had learned from watching Super Circus in the late forties. "The Super Circus guy was good, he was a plate man, I think, but I really only watched to see Mary Hartline. She was so beautiful with all that long blond hair. All I ever wanted before I met Bonamo was to be like Mary Hartline on Super Circus. I didn't make cheer-leaders at Loogootee till my senior year, because of my eyes, and even though I made pompom girls when I was a junior, I didn't really care about anything but having hair like Mary Hartline's, till I saw the great Bonamo with the Lorgan-Marar, that time in Indianapolis."

Bonamo paces through his Chelsea suite and opens the New Orleans metal-grille doors to the balcony and steps out into the cool New York air. He stares at the traffic on 23rd Street and the YMCA across the street. Dots joins him for a moment and slips her arm in his, and they listen to the fire-engine sirens on Eighth Avenue. "There are always fires on Eighth Avenue," Bonamo says. "And always, it seems, fire engines to service them."

"Once there was a fire in this hotel when we were here," Dots says casually, her gaze fixed on a policeman ticketing the cars parked along 23rd Street.

"And you grabbed our costumes and ran to the street. You grabbed the costumes, and I grabbed my silver-tipped cane."

"I only took what I could get."

"When I was younger I would have just run."

"Me too."

"Or perhaps when I was younger, I would have stayed to watch the fire. When I was younger—" Bonamo stops talking about the fire and comes back into the room. "I'll tell you a story about when I was young. When I was young the first great juggler I ever saw was Pierre Amara, who could juggle eight billiard balls and three white doves. If there had been a fire, Pierre would have saved those birds. He kept them in a cotton bag and fed them sedatives in their suet. They were so whoozy that Pierre could shower them and cascade them four or five times until they woke up and flew into the auditorium. The birds were so drugged they probably wouldn't have known there was a fire. They grew to like the spiked suet and so they would always fly back for more and make themselves ready for the next show. The stupid things never realized that what they loved so much was their undoing.

"I saw Pierre juggle the doves when I was a boy in Lübeck. At the time I did not speak to him, I was too scared. For years

I dreamed of juggling Amara's birds. I had visions of myself dressed in feathers, the plumage of pheasants and peacocks. I would draw doves from my throat and then juggle them until I joined them with my feathers, and we would fly together in a circle, a cascade of moving feathers, without a juggler. Years later, when Pierre and I were friends—colleagues—I told him of my seeing him in Lübeck and of my fear of speaking with him. But I never told him of my dream. Pierre could shower five balls in a right-hand direction and then, without pause or a stop reverse—absolutely no break in the motion—he could shower them in a left-hand direction. Just before his death he could keep nine balls in the air. Remarkable man, Pierre Amara. I still on occasion dream of his doves.

"From Pierre I learned to work out each day—even when I don't have a job. Pierre did it all his life, and I will do it all mine. Now, to me, an hour or so a day of basic ball work is like practicing scales, necessary, and even a small amount of pleasure in it. I use only juggling balls made of the finest boxwood and finished in bright colors, like billiard balls. I buy them, as Pierre did, a dozen at a time, from Carpatha's in London. Carpatha's only, and the hell with the rest. They come in small wicker hampers fitted out in cotton bunting and made by true craftsmen. Some artistes use billiard balls. I find them too heavy. With billiard one's palms sweat and it affects control. Some like tennis, others metal or hard rubber, but for me only balls from Carpatha's made of the finest boxwood, by true craftsmen."

Bonamo looks over Studio B of the Harlequin Rehearsal Hall, paces off the length of the room, breathing its crampedness, absorbing its dust. He springs slightly to check a loose floor tile, muttering, "Filthy, not fit for work." Dots, opening the wicker hamper where Bonamo keeps his rehearsal equipment, adds, "There's not near enough height for balls." Dots nervously tries to blow a coating of dust off the top of the old upright piano that fills one corner of Studio B. "Should I outten the big light?

That'll make less glare." Bonamo, ignoring her, looks up at the water-stained acoustical tile that forms the Harlequin's ceiling and then springs on the tile floor again. "Is there," Dots continues, "too much glare and not enough height for balls?"

Bonamo slips off his baggy black trousers to reveal white satin shorts with a red racing stripe and slits up the sides, meant to give breathing space to bulging thighs. Bonamo's thin hairy legs barely touch the material. Dots hands him a white velour jacket from the hamper. The jacket, cut like a high-school basketball team's warm-up uniform, zips up the back and is decorated with red stars. Bonamo wears it over his thin chest and lets it touch his delicate throat. His reedy frame looks lost in the expansive folds of velour. Across the back in red script it says:

THE GREAT BONAMO

Bonamo slips the jacket on and shakes his arms, pumping them, feeling the blood. He runs in place for a moment and rolls his neck, like a diver on the high board. As Bonamo shakes his muscles his frail form begins to look more muscular, more compact. One last flex of the fingers and he shouts, "Pull!" Dots tosses him a blue-and-white ball, and with a steady arching sweep he floats the ball into the air above him and brings his other hand into place to catch a second ball and then a third. As she throws she taps rhythm with her foot and sings in a delicate soprano.

> "Good night, Irene,
> Irene, good night,
> Good night, Irene, good night."*

Bonamo, picking up her tempo, and keeping the balls in the air, snarls, "Pull! Pull more fast." Dots increases the speed of her song and tosses a fourth, then a fifth ball to Bonamo, who increases the length of the throw. When all five balls are circling at once, Bonamo begins to add body spin and quick claps of the hands

* See copyright page.

between catches. As he claps, almost applauding himself, he screams like a Samurai warrior in battle, "Haai-ya—hee!"

As if desperate to be heard, Dots increases the volume of her song:

> "Irene, good night,
> I'll see you in my dreams. . . ."*

Then Bonamo changes the tempo of the song and sings with Dots:

> "Sometimes I live in the country,
> Sometimes I live in town. . . ."*

As Dots throws the sixth ball to Bonamo, one already in flight hits a loose-hanging, water-soaked Harlequin studio acoustical tile and all the balls fall down. Bonamo stops singing immediately and Dots stops a beat later.

"The ceiling. It hit the damned ceiling," he says angrily.

"It don't matter."

"That rhythm was superb. I could have gone faster. More balls, even."

"Don't worry, this place is too low a ceiling. This place is a dump."

"I was there—my hand was there, right on schedule, but the ball wasn't."

"It don't matter. You were going real good."

Dots, pleased with the praise of the rhythm, chases after the five balls, scooping them up and putting them back in the wicker hamper. Bonamo takes one of the balls between his thumb and forefinger and turns it slowly. "That doesn't happen very much any more. It really was the ceiling. I don't get mad. When I was younger, I would get furious if that would happen. I still get upset when something goes wrong in performance, but not so much any more in rehearsal. A rehearsal's a rehearsal, nothing more. I still am afraid of accidents on stage, of balls falling or of

* See copyright page.

slipping. When I was younger I dreamed of juggling fire, of throwing eggs and fire." Bonamo unzips his velour warm-up jacket, drapes it across his shoulders, and sits backward on a straight-back chair. Dots walks quickly to him and begins massaging his shoulders, kneading the flesh, then pushing the skin on his arms down toward his fingers, pushing the tension out to the floor. Bonamo rolls his neck slightly and Dots sings more of "Good Night, Irene" to him.

"I used to have accidents like that all the time—in rehearsals and performance. It was disaster followed by catastrophe. But after the war while I was traveling with the Bartok circus out west—just before I joined Lorgan-Marar—out on the coast —I had a flash, a whole vision of what juggling might be—could be, should be. I threw out all my old techniques, all the skill and procedure I had learned, everything, and from then on I began to work differently, more from within. Instead of following an image of what it might be, I began to sense its essence. I gave up on all the old techniques. Pierre had taught me the Continental system, all the old baroque European ways, cascades and shuffles, showers and endless sweeps. We worked for weeks on all the flashy things—cross overs and Spanish flourishes, French ducks and pins. I was always forever bouncing and bowing. I knew that for it to be true it must be a more subtle thing. Clearer, more delicate and precise. I knew what I had been doing was not so much artistry as showing off. I went inside myself to find the way to do it, instead of following the ways other people, even including Pierre, had done it. I quit Bartok and didn't perform in public for a very long time—almost seven months. It was like I couldn't juggle at all. I was thirty years old, had been juggling all my life, and it was like I couldn't juggle at all. I started completely over. I worked out every day. Not like this. All day. Ten hours a day some days. That's how you get to be the best."

Dots takes a white towel from the hamper and pats Bonamo's face and throat, caressing him with the Chelsea's faded terry cloth, and then starts to sing to him again.

"That's the only way to be the best in the world. And when I'm working right—really right—I feel like I am one beat ahead of the universe. One beat ahead of the whole rhythm of the universe. That's when I know I am the best there is, ever was, and ever will be. That's when I know I am the basis and the core, the conclusion of all juggling has ever been and ever will be, that I am the spirit and the mind of juggling. Juggling is my religion, and when I'm working right, when I feel the rhythm, I am the god. The crowds are my congregation and Dots is my priest."

Dots smooths his flat black thinning hair back and whispers, "Shush, Shush, shh," and moves her mouth very close to his ear:

> "Sometimes I live in the country,
> Sometimes I live in town,
> Sometimes I have a great notion
> To jump in the river and drown."*

Bonamo and Dots on Sunday night in the Chelsea's Don Quixote Bar and Spanish Restaurant, watching the Sullivan show. Dots smiles up at the Happy New Year banners, several months old, and Bonamo sits serenely sipping a Coca-Cola. Bonamo appeared regularly on Sullivan's program in the fifties, when it was called "Toast of the Town," and he now appears two or three times a year. He talks regularly with Sullivan's talent coordinators, who frequently check on his availability. Bonamo and Dots depend on the Sullivan appearances to stimulate bookings during the rest of the year. "Today the people all want to watch rock singers," he says. "Today's heroes are all rock heroes. Very few jugglers or real performers in the old style, acrobats, or your aerialist, or even the animal men, let alone jugglers, are heroes today. The young girls all follow the rock singers now. It used to be they went after jugglers. More for lion tamers and animal men, then came jugglers and magicians. After that they went for strong men. It will pass, and they'll want jugglers again. Like

* See copyright page.

olden times. In the Middle Ages, in the golden age of juggling, the juggler was king, and no competition from lion tamers."

Dots smiles and adds, "Sullivan will want us more too. Now he has jugglers just sometimes."

"And those are mostly comedy jugglers. I have no taste for comedy jugglers," Bonamo says. "Dressed like tramps, they cover up their lack of skill with jokes and pratfalls. Only W. C. Fields was both a great clown and a great juggler, and that was because he always kept his dignity. Other comedy jugglers have no dignity. Bill Fields was a great juggler, you know, before he got in the movies. Remarkable man, Bill Fields. All the stories you hear about him? Probably mostly true—but nevertheless, a truly fine juggler. A man of enormous dexterity and skill."

Dots says hesitantly, "He was mean to me. It's not nice to talk about the dead, but that man was never nice to me, not once."

"No, no," Bonamo says to her gently. "That was Forester the acrobat. Bill died when you were in high school. The thing was, even though he didn't like people very much, he really did like pretty girls. But they didn't like him very much. The girls always passed him by. He always hated that. I sometimes think Bill's life would have been easier, simpler, if a few of the pretty girls he had liked would have paid some attention to him. Girls thought he was interesting—after all, he was a movie star—but they couldn't ever really want him the way he wanted them. Poor Bill, all he ever really wanted was a pretty blond face and hips that moved back and forth."

"He made me scared," Dots adds quietly.

"Bill Fields once tried to teach a dog to juggle. He worked hard with that dog. At first the dog tried to eat the balls instead of throwing them. Bill used to kick the poor thing."

"That's what I mean. Imagine, a dog."

"Finally the dog could juggle a little, not really good enough to perform on a stage, but for a dog he was a good juggler. But by that time he was an old dog and right after he learned how, he died. He just got old and died."

"Poor thing," Dots adds. "He kicked it more than once too."

"Bill was an equilibrist as well; he could do remarkable balancing routines. Fields could juggle bottles like no one since Don Sylvester Lopez, the great Spanish aerialist and juggler. At his height he would use only champagne bottles. Fields could throw five Dom Pérignon bottles to the tune of 'Weel May the Keel Row.' His nose twitched at the sight of china on a mantelpiece."

Dots smiles, remembering Fields too. "It wasn't safe to invite him to your house if you had good china. Or even if you had bad china. If you had a house."

"I suppose he was mean. It is said that when Fields died, his last words were 'I have really loved children and dogs . . . on second thought, screw 'em.' Or some such. I have heard that story many times, all around the world. It is funny. Very ironic. He may have said that in his life and it would probably have pleased him to think that people thought those were his last words. But they weren't. He died on Christmas Day and I was there and his last words were very soft and he asked for his blue-and-white hard-rubber cane and then he reached for a woman who was standing there, but he was very pale then, and she was scared and stepped back. He said to her, 'Help me, help me.' When she moved away from he said, 'Oh no.' And then only tears. Those were his last words. 'Oh no.' I salute him, Bill Fields, old W.C. and his blue-and-white cane. He was a brilliant—I would say a juggler's juggler. I drink to him, and the girls who walked by."

Dots nudges Bonamo gently and points up at the television set. "It's time, Sullivan's going to be on."

"I left Lübeck to follow Pierre, before the trouble began in Europe. In the early thirties I guess it was. We were touring Germany. The government put a freeze on travel, on who could go where. We were in some little town in Bavaria—a village practically, and there we were. We couldn't leave, and we couldn't stay. The peasants didn't know what to make of it—a circus arrives and the glamour comes and goes before anyone knows what happened. You set up at night, do your tricks, juggle your balls, and leave before anyone knows what has happened. Except with the travel ban we were stuck. The people from the town got very nervous. They didn't like us hanging around; Bavarians like their jugglers and their acrobats under tents, or in rings, not walking down the street. So we began sneaking out— some of the people just disappeared, poof and they were gone. I was so young, I was never quite sure what was going on, politically I mean.

"Pierre woke me very early, about five in the morning I think, and we left. He and his wife, who was costume mistress for the circus, and I. We just walked across the border into Austria and that was that. The border was only a few miles away and it only took a few hours. Later Pierre established a story that we sneaked out inside a tuba and a big parade drum. It made a big splash in the papers and got on radio all over the world. It was to make a great deal of publicity and make us famous. It was to create a mystique and get us a job. It worked some— Pierre had visions of us being on the front pages for weeks, it didn't get that, but it was widely reported. In some papers it said I was Pierre's son, and I had been concealed inside a circus drum for several hours. Lottie, Pierre's wife, got carried away and said the drum was played by border guards, possibly damaging my eardrums for life. The story was quite thoroughly reported. *Paris-Match* kept asking for pictures of the drum, and it was in *Time* magazine and in the *Times*—the London *Times*. But really we just walked away. No one was guarding the border at all. With all the publicity from the big escape we got jobs right away. The headlines were very funny to us: 'Circus troupe escapes Nazis in daring escapade,' or some such. We wound up touring Austria and Switzerland and southern France until the war really got started.

"I was away from Europe for the whole war. I toured England and Scotland with the Gabor-Nagy circus, a little European traveler. We played for the troops, the RAF and the others. I was still learning, so I had other jobs besides being Pierre's apprentice. I had to clean up, work around. For a while I was a peg boy—I held the tent pegs while the roustabouts hammered them into the ground. I enjoyed it—the roustabouts were fat sweaty men and they cut their shirts off at the sleeves and some had purple tattoos on their muscles and they swore in six languages. But when Pierre saw me being peg boy he was afraid I'd damage my hands and not be able to juggle. So he got me transferred to selling peanuts and general clean-up. Pierre always said my hands were my fortune and I mustn't risk them. I was young enough to be able to do it. We spent most of the war trying to get out of England, or at least out of London. I was there for a little bit of the blitz.

"In nineteen-forty-four, finally, we got to the States. Pretty soon the war was over and then everybody could come, but at the time it was very hard to do. The Bartok toured this country and Canada for a few years. We were billed as the only European traveling circus in the U.S.A. It was very interesting in its way. I learned whatever I know about this country in those days. We played mostly one-week engagements all over the country—setting up on a Monday and playing through Sunday night. We traveled by truck and bus. In Ringling you have trains, but with Bartok it was only truck and bus. We carried our tents on our backs like a parade of turtles crawling all over the country. It was not bad for me; Pierre, as senior member of the troupe, and being married to the wardrobe mistress, had his own little trailer, and I had a little corner of it for myself. Most of the unmarried people slept in the back of a huge truck. A semi they called it. Semi terrible I call it. The sides of it were fitted out with bunks, six high, and the only air was by the door and the only privacy was in the dark. Mostly the grips and the roustabouts stayed in there. It smelled of stale liquor. Once when Pierre's wife was sick I had to stay there. I was frightened all night, but nothing

happened. In the morning I smelled of elephant dung and wet
rope.

"Right after that tour is when I met Dots, when we played
Indianapolis. There wasn't room for the two of us in Pierre's
trailer, and I don't think Lottie and Dots would have gotten on
anyway. So I put together our act. Pierre helped to design it. By
that time I was doing solo pieces anyway. And I was getting tired
of the circus—much more money to be made as a single. At first
we had second-rate jobs—carnivals and fairs, but pretty soon
we were playing Vegas. The Frontier Hotel, second billing in
the winter of nineteen-fifty or fifty-one. We played all over
in those days and made big money, real big money. It wasn't
easy—for every job in Vegas, or in the Garden, or on Sullivan
or Big Top we had to play a lot of lousy one-nighters."

Dots, in a blue pants suit, tight against the start of bulges in
her flesh, and carrying a bag of cosmetics and cookies, comes
in and listens quietly to Bonamo talking about Sullivan and Vegas
and the one-night stands. "We got a lot of money in Vegas," she
says. "And it was nice being out West, the air is so clean out
there. They're all talking about how bad the air is here now, well,
the air was always bad here. It's just that now everybody's always talking about it. But the real thrill was being on Sullivan.
My aunt in Indianapolis saw us and called up. It was the first
long-distance person-to-person phone call I ever got. It was also
the first one my aunt ever made. Sullivan was live in those days
and she called the television station in New York to see if I was
all right. The real thrill was being on that show. Sullivan named
us. Tell how he named us."

"I was billed as the Great Bonamo in Vegas, when Sullivan
saw me. He was on a trip out west, scouting talent, and he caught
my act. I knew he was in the house so I really laid it on."

"I switched into my best costumes," Dots says. "Between
numbers I changed. I had to rush. My blue with the red silk, and
then my white."

"I did a double shower with some very complex and subtle cascades, and also all my cane routines. It was a very fine show—one of the best I've ever given, and when it was over Sullivan came up on the stage of the Frontier Hotel and shook my hand and said to me in front of the entire audience and the management and the entertainment director, 'You are the world's greatest juggler.' Then he invited me on his show."

Bonamo and Dots packing their trunk, to leave New York for Burton, Ohio, where they'll play the Geauga County Fair. Packing their sandalwood balancing poles, silver-tipped canes, and boxwood balls, folding Bonamo's blue silks and Dots' red-trimmed tutus, easing their way to a cab for the ride to Grand Central and the train to Ohio. "I used to take the Twentieth-Century Limited to go out west. It always left from the same track, track thirty-four at Grand Central, and I sat in the observation car, which was always the last car on the train. They always gave me a newspaper with breakfast and a carnation for my lapel. Now I guess you take whatever train they give you."

"Ringling's bought the observation car from the Limited," Dots says. "The manager lives in it all by himself, I heard. Or it's his office or something. That's Ringling's for you."

"Now of course it's all flying," Bonamo says, almost sadly.

"We fly sometimes."

"Sometimes. But the train is easier when you're going somewhere not near an airport. I have a slight aversion to flying. I think its the result of having been in London during the blitz. It is one thing to throw small objects, missiles, into the air and quite another to be attached to those missiles. I don't mean to say I am afraid of flying, just skeptical. To have been in London during the blitz, even part of it, makes one skeptical of all other problems and difficulties, particularly airborne ones. To have had fire rained down on your head nightly, as a matter of course, is to inure one to lesser problems."

Bonamo stops talking and opens the trunk that Dots has just finished packing. He touches his blue silks and his white

velour warm-up jacket and then looks at the tiny hampers of juggler's balls and runs his long fingers across the bumps of the
wicker. Dots starts to tell him to hurry, and then thinks better
of it. She rubs his shoulders and whispers to him softly. Bonamo's
hands quiver and he sits on the edge of the Chelsea's bed, draw-
ing his knees tightly together, drumming his heels on the floor,
his blue silks in his lap. "What do they know of jugglers in the
West? Of Sullivan and the Garden, what do they know?" he
asks. Dots takes Bonamo's velour warm-up jacket from the trunk
and drapes it over his shoulders. "I am the world's greatest juggler. I have juggled with Amara and danced with Fields; per-
formed with Morimoto, the Oriental who juggled his own ex-
creta and swallowed his nose. I have the mystique of greatness.
The Great Bonamo. The world's greatest juggler in the world."

Dots begins to sing to him, softly, soothingly into his ear. The
sounds wash over him as beads of sweat on his forehead drip
down and collect in the black curly hairs on his arms.

> "Good night, Irene,
> Irene, good night,
> Good night, Irene,
> I'll get you in my dreams. . . ."*

Bonamo shakes his wrists and flexes them as if he were juggling.
"Bonamo, Bonamo, Bonamo. Greatest juggler in the world," he
says as he pretends to throw champagne bottles in the air.

> Sometimes I live in the country
> Sometimes I live in town*

"The only Bonamo they know is Bonamo's Turkish Taffy."

> Sometimes I have a great notion*

"Bonamo from a box. But my tricks are real. All real genuine
tricks and no faking. It is my juggler's mystique. Pierre always
said a juggler without a mystique was like a horse without a rider.

* See copyright page.

I play Sullivan three times a year and that man has given me his word that I will always play his show three times a year if I care to. And I care to. I most certainly do. I could cascade an endless shower of Turkish taffy boxes. Send them into the air, a geyser of Turkish taffy boxes, and arrest their endless flight, their collective Turkish taffy flight at whatever point I chose to: Bonamo, the world's greatest juggler."

"And Dots," she whispers in his ear.

"And Dots. And Dots. Bonamo, the world's greatest juggler, and Dots."

To jump in the river and drown*

Dots drops his blue silks back into the trunk and brushes his hair away from his eyes. "We have to get the train out to Ohio. For the concert. C'mon or we'll miss it."

As the porter arrives to take their trunks down to a waiting cab Bonamo clutches Dots' arm, and just before they leave for the elevator he says, "In Ohio, at the fair, during our concert performance, we will do showers and cascades. We will do our entire show, with no stops. It is Ohio only and not Sullivan, or Vegas, but we will do it all. They are an audience and they will see Bonamo perform."

"That'll be good practice, too."

"Dots," Bonamo says, pushing back his shoulders and smoothing his hair, "Dots, Pierre Amara once gave me a piece of advice. He said to me, 'The one thing you must never do, my Bonamo, is you must never ever keep your audience waiting.' That's what Pierre said to me and that man could juggle five doves and keep nine balls in the air. He was the finest man and juggler I ever knew." And then Bonamo and Dots and the Chelsea porter take the elevator down to 23rd Street and the cab.

* See copyright page.

SING ALONG SID

Sing Along Sid, Prince of Tin Pan Alley and song-knower to the stars, moves through the Brill Building's fluorescent corridors, pushing his way into the elevator where Muzaked Mantovani, playing "The Man Who Got Away," floats him nine flights down from the offices of the Music Society of America and into the street. In the Broadway sun Sid snaps airplane-pilot sunglasses into place and smooths his pale rose Indian scarf, letting it fall casually across a plum-colored shirt. He rubs the narrow creases of his throat, straightens his silver G-clef cufflinks, hums a private song enriched with whistled trills, and heads for a bench in Bryant Park and a twenty-minute listening break. In the park, Sid spreads his bony frame across a stone bench, fishes a tape-mended transistor radio from his briefcase, and flips across the dial hunting for music, for unfamiliar melodies or new lyrics. He listens intently, without laughing, without enjoyment, until he hears the new or the unfamiliar: once through and the sound is etched in his head. Sid may forget the words, but a tune once heard is filed, ready at any time to tumble up from his throat in a soft breathy tenor.

Knower of songs, whistler of tunes, and graduate of the "college of musical knowledge," Sid moves easily through the web of music publishers and record promoters entrenched in the Brill Building's Tin Pan corridors, checking ancient melodies, mediating copyright disputes, or offering opinions when promoters or producers smell plagiarism in a melody or a lyric: Sid is a song-knower, the song-knower—encyclopedic song expert —available free-lance or on exclusive contract, adviser to the frantic, contestant to the many, composer to the few, and song-knower to the stars.

In addition to free-lancing among the music publishers and record promoters, Sid works each afternoon from one to four at the Music Society of America (MSA). Sid gets a small salary to sit in MSA's Brill Building offices, offering what the music business accepts as the definitive opinion and final judgment in all musical disputes. Each day MSA receives anxious phone calls about rights or lyrics to obscure, almost forgotten songs. Sid listens to the usually frantic callers, who hum a few bars and then ask hopefully if the song is in the public domain. Sid's office is a corner of the legal department, where at a long flush door table he sips tea with lemon from a cardboard container, returns the morning calls, punching the buttons on his phone and switching his singers from hold to the record room to the legal department.

"Listen, this is Professor S. at DesMoines College—I'm head of student activities here—"

"Yeah, what is it?" Sid runs a finger along the paper rim of his tea, shifts his long legs, drumming his foot on the floor.

"The student council is putting on an original musical comedy—*Sail! Sail!*—that's the name of it. It's tying up the whole campus—"

"What is it?" Sid cuts him off.

"We wrote some of the songs—the students did. Most of them. But some of the others, we'd like to know if we have to pay royalties or something on some of them—one of them."

"What is it?"

"I beg your pardon?"

"Gimme the song. The name. What's it called? You know, the title?"

" 'White Waters.' That's what we call it. But that's the thing. We wrote the lyrics—the students did. But the melody, the tune, is old. Everybody's heard it before. We don't want any trouble."

" 'White Waters,' huh?" Sid pokes through his mental files for an earlier use of the title.

"All we want is the melody and if we have to pay royalties or not."

"Sing it."

"What?"

"Sing. 'White Waters.' Sing it."

"On the phone?"

"Yeah. Sing it."

"I'm not a musician. I mean I could get the music director if you want—he's a music major. I don't always get it on pitch."

"Sing it."

"White Waters, white waters, we're goin' cross those foamy—"

"Those your lyrics?"

"I told you I'm not a musician. I'm the student activities—"

"You wrote 'em?"

"Some of the students did."

"Just hum the melody."

"Dah, dah-dah, dumm, de dah. Dah, dah, dum de dah . . . Ahh, that's all I can remember. I didn't expect to have to sing to you."

"Do the first part again."

"Dah, dah-dah, dumm, de dah."

Sid drums his knuckles on the hollow core table, flexes his shoulders, and bobs his head in rhythm, reaching for the sound. He cuts off his questioner. "And then it goes, Taa, rah, raa, de dum, dum dum?"

"That's it. That's it. Taa, taa, ba taaa!"

Sid smiles and croons with him. "Ba, baa taa. That's 'Singin' to My Baby.' Jack Kaplan and Maury Willis, around nineteen-thirty-four. I'll switch you to legal."

"Thank you very much. If you ever get out this way—"

Sid punches the white button at the base of his phone, swallows his cooling tea, and takes another call.

When television was younger and Sid was a star, he spent a spring amazing America as the all-time champion contestant on "Name That Tune." Sid lasted for weeks, beating the competition cold and running up winnings of thousands of dollars.

Sid was "Name That Tune" champ, and everyone acknowledged that he knew more songs than any of his opponents—"Everybody said I knew the most in the history of the show—Cullen and the producer and everybody said it. Only I'm not too good on running, I'm lousy on coordination, I admit it. So I lost out." There's a trace of sadness in Sid's voice as he recalls the show: "There were two contestants. You both wore U.S. Keds—they gave 'em to you to wear—and when the song started, if you knew it—you raced the other guy up and pulled this rope and rang a bell. First guy to ring the bell with the right answer won. So I lost out." Sid stops talking, perhaps to recall his season in the sun, the fan letters and the crowds, or maybe Bill Cullen. He stretches his long arms in front of him, as if he were conducting a silent orchestra. He smiles and wipes the beads of sweat that dot his long throat. "They should of made it just on songs that you know, not on how you could run. Then I could of kept on winning forever. What's running got to do with it anyway? I'm a song-knower. Half the reason they put that running stuff in there was so they could have a way of beating somebody who was otherwise unbeatable. Me." Sid begins his shadow conducting again, reaching out to his private orchestra as if it were floating away, tapping rhythm with his foot. "They had to get some young guy who could run like crazy to beat me. I'm not saying it was fixed, but it's funny that the only other guy in the history of "Name That Tune" who knew all the songs was a young guy who could run like crazy. But I'm not bitter."

Sid was born in Brooklyn, in an apartment in Bensonhurst. As his parents prospered—his father was an insurance salesman —the family moved to a large duplex on Ocean Avenue. With the house came an old Baldwin upright piano. Sid was seven when he arrived at the house on Ocean Avenue and the Baldwin was the first piano he ever touched. "I started in banging on it right away—my mother saw me at the ivories and it was lessons from then on." In those days, the twenties, Sid's parents could afford to import a piano teacher to the house, three afternoons a week. "She was there when I got home from school every Tuesday, Thursday, and Friday. Miss Rosa was her name. She called me Siddie. She was a great big Italian lady with bosoms that smelled like sheet music. We used to drill all the time." Sid smiles softly and fingers an imaginary keyboard, singing the song every piano boy knows:

> "Papa Haydn's
> Dead and gone,
> But his memory
> Lingers on."

Sid laughs, and plays the imaginary keys again. "That's the first thing I ever learned. It's really by Haydn." He fingers the melody again. "C-C-E-E-G-G-E. By Haydn." Sid's piano lessons lasted till he was in the ninth grade, when Miss Rosa got married and moved to Staten Island. "I studied with Miss Rosa for seven years—I just couldn't get used to any other teacher. She always wore these wool suits, and when I was learning the keyboard she used to reach across me to move my arm and I could feel the wool. I can still feel it sometimes. When I was learning the pedals, her foot came down on mine. I used to dream about her, Miss Rosa. About how we would open a little piano store. I wanted to touch her bosoms so badly, I used to almost cry about it. I used to fake all kinds of reasons to accidentally touch 'em. They were spongy. I used to dream about 'em. Like they weren't really bosoms at all, but actually a big keyboard. The nipples were pedals and the black keys were like little moles and I would play everything she ever taught me, perfectly. That's how I learned so much piano: I was always imagining Miss Rosa's bosoms. I tried going to some guy, but it just wasn't the same. Besides, it was the depression and we had to economize."

When Sid was in high school he played the piano at parties and student gatherings. "There was this ad in all the magazines then," he recalls. " 'They laughed when I sat down to play the piano.' You know, 'Learn to play the piano and be popular.' Well, it was kind of true. I was skinny and I wasn't good at sports—I didn't even like sports—and that meant you were dead at Eastern. But I could play the piano. So I would go to parties and when I couldn't get any girls I could always sit at the piano. It wasn't like an excuse—it was like for the good of the party. Afterwards, when the kids—the boys—were talking about what girls they got, I had a legitimate excuse: I was at the piano. I used to imagine that I was in a Western movie—that we weren't really at a party on Ocean Avenue, but out West and I was the piano player in the saloon with swinging doors. I was even going to get those little garters for my sleeves. My father wore 'em, and I was going to borrow them to wear. I would have a big mug of cold beer on my piano and the girls would take time out to come over and see how the piano player was doing."

After high school Sid went to Brooklyn College for what turned out to be a short stay. He lived at home, declared himself a pre-law student, and made extra money playing in supper clubs in Manhattan. After his first year at Brooklyn, Sid got a summer job as back-up piano man on a cross-country tour with Harry Abramson and his orchestra. "We played all the hell over —we were supposed to be only out for the summer, but I was with Harry for a year and a half." While he was touring Sid wrote his first songs. "We'd be out on the road somewhere, some little college or country club, you traveled by train in those days, and since I never wanted to practice—hell, I was playing four or five hours a night—I'd just sit at my machine and plunk— little riffs, just to see what would happen. Pretty soon it'd be a song. The lyrics would be natural—my mood, or about New York, you know."

Sid claims to have written hundreds of songs. He has copyrighted two dozen, and several were published in the late thirties and early forties. Although he has never had a really big hit, a few of his songs have been recorded. "Muzak picked up 'Cry Baby,' you might remember that, I wrote it in about thirty-nine. Muzak bought it a few years ago. Every now and then you hear it in an elevator or a bank somewhere. They pay peanuts, Muzak."

During World War II Sid was in Special Services, playing the piano with service orchestras. He spent most of the war in the United States, but he did make one tour of Europe. "It's funny," he recalls, "I was only in Europe, but the songs I wrote for the war were all about the Japs. I never understood that. One thing was I guess more words rhymed with Jap than with German. For German you got vermin, but that's about it." One of Sid's war songs, "Beat 'Em Cold," was recorded by Jungle Jim Jackson on Decca in 1943 and was mildly popular in the States. It won Sid a letter of commendation from President Roosevelt. The melody was a variant of the Eastern High School pep song. *Stars and Stripes* said the song had rousing lyrics:

> Screams, Marines,
> Hit those Japs,
> Bring freedom back,
> Fight 'em bold,
> Fight 'em bold,
> Beat 'em cold.

The letter, framed and dusted regularly, hangs in Sid's apartment next to his certificates of membership in the MSA and the Song Writers Guild. Sid doesn't write songs any more, or at least not for recording or publication. He dabbles occasionally, but he hasn't seriously tried to put a song together since "Name That Tune."

After "Name That Tune" Sid was a consultant on the "Sing Along with Mitch" show, for a short time. "My job was to think up songs that people would like to sing along with. I gave 'em a lot of songs and they paid me for it—plenty, too—but after that they didn't need me again, or something. I tried to get in with Schirmer's Music Publishers—you know, help 'em out, suggest what songs should go in song books—those 'Songs around the Campfire' books they put out? There's lots better songs could be in there than what they use."

Sid doesn't collect records himself, but he does have a rather extensive collection of sheet music, some of it quite rare, dating back to the 1870s. He keeps it all in stacks and drawers in his apartment, a large room on West 46th Street. Sid's room is two flights above, appropriately enough, a music store. "For a while a few years ago when I was broke—before I got the gig at MSA —I worked in the music store downstairs, but I didn't like it— the pay was lousy—it's idiot work and they expected me to clean up the stock room. No thanks, I'll sell music and records to people—that's honest work, but I'm no janitor. I was a TV star once, I'm not cleaning up any back rooms." Sid stops talking and stares at the pigeons fluttering through Bryant Park. He picks up a handful of pebbles and tosses them one by one to to the birds, which waddle over and peck at them as if the stones were food. Sid laughs at a particularly persistent pigeon which keeps nibbling at a bright blue stone. Sid tosses another, directly at the bird, and watches it disappear into the smog above 42nd Street.

"I heard 'Name That Tune' might get back on the air. Why not? They're putting 'I Got A Secret' back on. Why not 'Name That Tune'? The thing was the ratings. It had lousy ratings. But the fans were very loyal. Your 'Name That Tune' fan was a real fan—maybe there weren't so many of them, but they really watched. If you were a network or a sponsor, who would you rather have, a whole bunch of fans who only watched casually, or not so many who really watched? Which would you rather? Of course you want the real tight fan—if you have any sense. And 'Name That Tune' fans were tight. I got fan mail from these people—it was fantastic. At the height, when I was going into my seventh week, I got almost as much mail as Cullen himself. They were going to give me my own dressing room and everything. If it comes back I might be on the staff—not just a contestant, but like one of the producers—you know, picking the songs, interviewing the contestants. They saw after a while that I knew more songs than anybody." A last pigeon stares at the pile of pebbles near Sid's foot and cautiously waddles over. Sid stops talking and stares at the gray bird. The pigeon, perhaps emboldened by Sid's silence, inspects the pebbles. Sid raises his arm as if to strike the bird but instead sings softly:

"You are my sunshine,
My only sunshine,
You make me happy
When skies are gray."*

The bird stares at Sid, bobs its head, flaps its wings, and then lifts itself into the air. As it spins up toward the library Sid throws his last stone at it with sudden viciousness and then finishes his song:

"The other night, dear,
As I lay sleeping,
I dreamed I held you in my arms.
When I awoke, dear, I was mistaken,
And I hung my head and cried.*

"I know that's not the greatest thing in the world, to know all the songs—but I'm still proud of it. I mean I know it's better to invent a cure for cancer, but still you can't deny that what I do I do better than anybody. And I'm sorry, but that's something to be proud of. For a while I was gonna get on 'The Sixty-Four-Thousand-Dollar Question.' They were interviewing me and everything—they started getting the questions set, but then all that stuff about it being fixed came out. They never said anything to me about it being fixed—maybe they would've if I'd gotten on the show. But I wouldn't have done it. I'm a song-

* See copyright page.

knower. I'm as good as I am and no better. If there was one I
didn't know, I'd admit it, right on television, prime time double A,
in front of ten million people. You cheat, you're nothing. How do
you think those people feel now? That professor who cheated?
Never. I either know, or I go down to defeat like a man. Like a
song-knower."

Sid is really an expert on pop—he knows a lot of rock and
a lot of blues and folk too, but his own taste, and his area of
real expertise, is night-club pop—love songs, torch songs, comedy numbers, the stuff families like to listen to. "I like rock and
roll and all that—but the kids, they go a little overboard for it.
It'll pass. It used to be Sinatra and Tony Bennett, then Elvis and
the Beatles. Now the new ones, Tom Jones, all of 'em. The only
different part is with rock and roll these days they publish books
—you could always buy lyrics—I was a charter subscriber to
Lyric Magazine when it was out and all the kids used to buy the
pop sheets, but nobody called it "poetry of rock" or whatever
the hell it is. I mean I looked at Dylan's lyrics—and I looked
close. It's good stuff, don't get me wrong, the kid can write
lyrics, I got a lot of respect for that. And some of the others,
too. But I don't see where they get off calling that stuff the
greatest poetry since Shakespeare. You look at the stuff Jimmy
Scammo was doing when Dylan was in short pants—I don't see
why that's not considered poems. If Bob Dylan's stuff is poems,
why not Jimmy's? Or Jack Goldberg's? Christ, Jack Goldberg
wrote beautiful songs. Beautiful stuff." Sid jumps up, excited,
an idea bursting from him. He grabs his Indian scarf and pulls
on it, running it through his fingers. "Look, why not 'The Poetry
of Jimmy Scammo?" A book of Jimmy's lyrics. I'll edit it. I'll
get a publisher. Maybe Schirmer's—I used to work there—I
know those guys. Or maybe one of the big houses—Random
House, maybe. 'The Poetry of Jimmy Scammo.' Or Jack Goldberg. It could be a series. All the late greats. Kids'll love it. It'll

sell a million copies. A gold book. I could edit a whole series of gold books. Million sellers." Sid clears his throat and sings softly, almost sensuously, in a smoky tenor:

"Our love is crumblin',
I'm in a lovin' daze,
Our love is crumblin',
I'm in a lovin' haze."

Sid winds up, throws his arms back the way the big stars do at the Persian Room, and belts out the finale:

"And my heart is where,
Oh yes my heart is where
The cold wind blooows.

That's Jimmy Scammo—nineteen-thirty-nine. Beautiful stuff." Sid clears his throat again, about to do another number, but sits instead, stretching his neck and pushing his shoulder blades back. "Course it's true those guys only did lyrics. Dylan does lyrics and music, plus he sings them too. He's a triple threat, Dylan. That's something."

Every morning at nine-thirty Sid shuts off his wind-up alarm clock and flicks on his bedside radio. He immediately begins spinning the dial at random from one station to the next, listening to the morning music, his inner ear always privately listening for one of his own melodies. "A lot of writers use other guys' melodies—hell, that's what I'm at MSA for. A lot of theft goes on and nothing happens. 'Hello, Dolly' was in a big lawsuit. I was called in on that. And some senator out west—Bayh was his name—was in a mess over the melody to his campaign song. It worked one year, so the next year the other guy bought the rights to it so this Bayh couldn't use it. I was called in on that. I know some tunes nobody did anything about. There was a song from a show—a big hit—it was a dead copy for 'Just a Love

Nest,' the theme song from 'Fibber McGee and Molly.' Everybody knew it. They made some chord changes and got away with it. I'll hear one of my own some morning and look out. I'll sock a lawsuit on 'em in multiple millions. Yes sir. Multiple millions."

Sid listens to the radio for an hour, switching from WNEW to WOR to WABC, avoiding disc-jockey chatter, searching for pure music as he sips his morning tea. By ten-thirty he begins dressing, in one of the colored music-business body shirts he favors. He pushes his thinning hair over his bald spot and walks to the Variety Rehearsal Studios on 56th Street. On the trip uptown, Sid stops to look at the stacks of yellowed scores of forgotten Broadway musicals in the window of the Quarter Note Music Store on Seventh Avenue. Sid pauses in front of the window long enough to point out that the Quarter Note hasn't changed its windows in three years. As he walks uptown on Seventh Avenue, Sid considers his future. "I might be on TV as a song-knower. I'd like to get on the talk shows. Just sit and talk about old songs and song-knowing. A lot of people remember me from 'Name That Tune,' and there's so many talk shows now they need a lot of guests. Merv, Johnny, David Frost, Cavett, plus all the daytime ones—the daytime ones are good to start with. I could break in with Cullen—like on 'Name That Tune' we worked well together—move up to Mike Douglas or the Today Show, then, when I'm in tight with NBC, on to Carson. Maybe get my own show—nothing big—even Channel 13— the Sing Along Sid show. Couple nights a week. No prime time."

Sid picks up a few dollars playing the piano for auditions at the Variety Arts. "Couple bucks now and then. Pocket money in case I have to take a publisher or an agent to lunch." In the Variety Arts, up a dirty flight of stairs, beyond a broken coffee machine, Sid sits, two or three mornings a week, awaiting the call. He doesn't usually have to wait long. The young men and women who want to be stars frequently show up for their auditions without an accompanist. Sid, for a fee, will rescue them.

A nervous young man pokes an effeminate head of blond curls out the door to Studio B and looks desperately at Sid, who is sitting on a crumbling red-leather couch, glancing through an old copy of *Newsweek*.

"Can you play?" he lisps at Sid, pulling a sheepskin vest tight against him.

"I can play anything." Sid closes the magazine and walks casually into the studio. The producer, grinning in a bright green Cassini suit, ignores him, while the music director, a fat, red-jowled man in a double-breasted blazer, fumbles with a stack of pictures and résumés of other aspirants to show-biz glamour.

The young man, clutching at his vest, whispers into Sid's ear, "Can you play 'On a Clear Day' in C?"

"Five bucks." Sid smiles as he nods yes he can play.

The singer looks dismayed and spins around to confront the producer, who is no longer there, and sputters at the music director, "I thought you had one here."

"An accompanist is your obligation," the music director answers as he buries his head in the pictures and résumés in front of him.

"I can't afford this." The young man bites his lip. "The prices are outrageous. How do I know this isn't a con game? I mean, what if I don't get the job?"

"You want to sing *a capella*?" The producer materializes next to the piano, sipping a can of Fresca. "But please decide, because there are some other people we need to hear—"

"No, no. You sure you know 'On a Clear Day'?"

"In C." Sid plays the first few bars standing up, whistling along with himself.

"I have sheet music." The singer shoves the pages onto the piano as Sid slides into place on the bench. "Light on the pedal and don't get ahead of me," he snaps.

The producer widens his grin. "Okay then, we all set?"

"All set," from Sid.

The young man loosens his shirt, shakes his arms like a basketball player at the foul line, and begins to audition:

> "On a clear day,
> rise and look around you,
> On a clear day . . ."

He turns to Sid, snaps his fingers impatiently, and throws a pleading look to the music director, who straightens the stack of pictures and résumés. Sid presses on the pedal and picks up the tempo.

> "You can see forever,
> and ever-more."

By noon, two auditions later and fifteen bucks richer, Sid leaves the Variety Arts, hails a cab for the ride back downtown to the MSA offices. The cab's radio is turned to WOR. Sid listens to the driver sing along with the radio as Connie Stevens sings "Guess Who I Saw Today." As the song ends, the driver's voice trails off a beat ahead of Connie's.

Sid looks up at the driver. "You like that song? 'Guess Who I Saw Today'?"

"I heard better. It's all right."

"You know who wrote that song? Murry Grand wrote that song, nineteen-fifty-two. That's who."

"Yeah?"

"Yeah. Murry Grand."

The driver pulls up in front of the Brill Building, kills the meter, chews on his toothpick, and as Sid is getting out of the cab says, "Murry Grand, huh?"

"Yep."

"How do you know?"

"Murry Grand. I know." Sid hands him a dollar, smiles a keep-the-change smile, and walks into the Brill Building elevator that will take him up to the MSA offices where he'll handle the morning phone calls.

R AT CLUB X

In the city of splendor, of famous waiters and forgotten millionaires, R stands on 7th Street and hunts for a taxi. His adrenalin pumping like legs in silent movies that run but never tire, R carries his Eclair—the hand-held, shoulder-mounted extension of his eye—on his lap as he travels up Sixth Avenue to the electronic bacchanal, there to join the coaxial prank and further his life in art.

R steps out of the elevator into the top-floor loft of a ware-house on 24th Street and walks past a stack of packing crates, nodding to Angelo, who waits by the door to collect the $5 per man that the $5 men will offer each hour and a half until nine o'clock tonight. R brushes past the black curtains that divide the room, and straightens his red velour pants, stretches his shoulders beneath his white wool sweater, and prepares the Eclair. "You can shoot anywhere and get anything with an Eclair, they cost plenty and they're worth it." Holding the camera under his arm, cradled like a child, R polishes the lens in steady circles, staring into the camera's eye as he works. He runs three drops of oil into the mechanism and then dusts the case with a tiny chamois. The girl he will photograph is lounging on the bed, smoking a cigarette. She watches R minister to the camera and nods to him.

"If I can get the capital," R says, "I'm going to do an entire stag flick like Kubrick in *2001*, all floating in space. It'll take fifty thousand dollars. The guys running this might go in on it. Angelo knows 'em. Sounds like a lot, but it's not. In pictures, fifty thousand dollars is nothing. *Tora Tora* cost twenty-five million. You imagine what kind of stag flicks you could make with that? And how many? You could make one for every five hundred people in the country. Angelo figured it out. But that's not what I'd do with that kind of bread. I'd put it on display. All twenty-five million in a glass case and charge people a buck to

look at it. I'd tour it around the country, all the major cities.
You'd make more money than Zanuck made on *Tora Tora* and
I'd film the people looking. At the twenty-five million. A *cinéma
verité* of people lined up to pay a buck to look at twenty-five
million. That's where the picture is in *Tora Tora*."

R has been resident film-maker at Club X for five weeks.
He shoots six shows a day, six days a week, and on Sunday
he rests. He is responsible for renting the camera and for placing
the club's weekly ads in *Screw* magazine and the *New York Re-
view of Sex*.

LIVE

SEE STAG FILMS

BEING MADE

LIVE

R is paid $150 per week and $25 for expenses. Angelo, who
hired him, pays him in cash each Friday after the last show. Although R is not responsible for hiring actors, he has made it
clear to Angelo that if he can't work with a performer he or she
is not to be rehired. R's favorite actors are a husband-and-wife
team who work two days a week. R feels he does his best work
with them. "They respond to my directions the best," he says.
R has been interested in films since he was a child. He grew up
in New Jersey and began playing with cameras before he was
seven. He is twenty-two and has made three shorts, as well as
assisting on several feature-length stag films. R got his Club X
job when a friend who had been doing it got drafted.

The girl, sipping her coffee, appears again and tells R that
the man hurt her with his elbow yesterday, during the last show.
"He kept jabbing me with it," she says. "I'm black and blue." R
says he will speak to him about it, then he tells her that her work
with her legs and arms was good, very smooth. She nods.

"The thing is, you can show stag flicks in the city now, so

it's logical that you can make them in the city. That's what we're doing. We throw our set open to the public while we're doing it. Cops can't touch us." R turns to the girl, who is wearing a bright yellow robe and smoking another cigarette. She asks for someone to turn on the heat. R tells her to speak to Angelo. "There was a write-up about us in the *Times*," R says. "It didn't stress the movie-making too much. It was a wrap-up of a couple of clubs. But we're the only one with any real equipment or know-how. That place over in the Wurlitzer Building, the director doesn't know beans. He's using an 8mm Bolex. Man, that's home movies. They have good casting, though. A couple of places on Eighth Avenue do some interesting work, but they're very sloppy."

Beyond the bed, on the other side of the black curtains, Angelo admits the first of the $5 men, for the noon show. The man wears glasses with clear plastic frames, a dark green wash-and-wear business suit that bags at the knees, and a narrow brown tie. He looks like a bookkeeper or perhaps a bank clerk. The man pokes his face through a peephole in the curtain, and then other eyes appear at other peepholes.

R speaks quietly to the girl. "Don't worry so much about movement today," he says. "Stay in the down light as much as you can. I want to do some Fritz Lang things the first show." She says nothing and steps out of her robe and sprawls naked across the bed, like an odalisk. R lines up a shot and takes a practice walk, panning from behind. The girl's partner enters in a hurry, apologizing for being late. R says nothing, but scowls as the man steps out of his dungarees and work shirt and hurries to join the woman on the bed. He is about twenty-five, slightly older than the girl. Angelo comes backstage and says "Okay, you could do it now," then goes in front of the curtain to make certain that none of the $5 men are using more than one peephole and that none are smoking. R dims the lights, turns on the Eclair, and steps upstage of the bed and says, "We are rolling and action." The girl stretches her legs and arms. Her partner caresses her and kisses her breasts. They roll about on the bed, changing positions, standing, then sitting. She begins to breathe loudly, then to moan. R moves in close, adjusting his lens and, speaking softly, almost whispering, says, "That's nice, very nice. Slurp it up, that's it. Turn to me, roll to me, slowly, slowly." As R speaks, the performers follow his instructions, moaning, caressing each other, and changing positions. "Nice, that's very nice," he says. "Stay in the light. Oh yeah, that's it, that's fantastic. Oh baby, it's amazing. Ummmmmm. Stay in there. To me. To me. Now push it. PUSH IT PUSH IT UMM-MMMMMMM." R begins to sweat as he speaks louder, standing over the bed, his Eclair whirring in the soft light, the sounds echoing in the high ceilings and through the loft's open space. On the other side of the curtain the $5 men stand in the dark, their faces pressed to the rough black fabric, eyes jammed in peepholes, staring silently, unblinkingly, at the bed. "Come on! Come on! Come on in!" R climbs up onto the end of the bed, straddling the couple, and shoots downward, an aerial shot of the snarl of arms and legs. He bobs the camera up and down, catching their rhythm, then dominating and accelerating it. "Oh yeah, oh yeah, pound it, do it, do it, fantastic." The woman begins to yell and the man to groan. R crouches down on top of the bodies and shoots a close-up of her face, writhing with his camera, in time with her hips. "Now pound it, POUND IT, POUND IT NOW," R screams, contorting his face and pushing the Eclair between them as the man collapses on top of his partner. R says, "Whew," wipes his forehead and steps down off the bed, smiling, slaps the man on the rump, pinches the girl, and says quietly, "Nice. That was nice. Take ten and we'll try it again, from another angle." As the couple goes back to their dressing area, R turns the lights on and Angelo tells the $5 men, "That's all, it's over. Everybody out. Next show, one-thirty." Huddled in their dark suits, newspapers and briefcases pressed to their waists, they file out quickly.

Between shows R relaxes behind the black curtains, sipping a can of diet cola. "I look at this as good practice," he says. "The way the unions have it all sewed up, you can't break into pictures. This stuff isn't going to win any Oscars, but some of it's actually pretty good. That stuff we just shot now was only so-so. I was trying some new ideas with the lights. The one-thirty I'm going to try for a Von Sternberg halo effect. I wasn't actually shooting this time, there wasn't any actual film in the camera. I use actual film when there's a cop in the audience. Angelo tells me. That clutches me. I do my best work in a dry run. When I have a good cast, it makes all the difference in the world."

Angelo parts the curtains and steps up onto the platform in front of the bed. "Twenty-seven," he says. "Not bad, we'll do thirty-five at three o'clock. You want coffee? Box office is buying."

R nods yes and Angelo leaves.

R looks out through the black linen curtains to watch the next audience gather. "We might be able to sell the film rights to that story in the *Times*. I'm not sure, the lawyers'll have to look it over. Zanuck had to buy the rights to Pearl Harbor for *Tora*. We wouldn't get that much, but we don't need as much. That write-up in the *Times* should get us some interest." The boy joins R and takes a sip of his coffee. R compliments him on his performance and tells him to watch his elbows.

Angelo comes backstage, smiling, and says, "Thirty-six. Sold out." R nods his approval and tells the boy and girl, "Stay in the cross-lighting more, let it wash over you." The boy nods and says okay. Then Angelo pats the girl on the rump, smiles again, and says, "Okay, you could do it now."

FAT BERNIE

The day of the Broadway column is over. Interest today is in the cultural scene; good theatre, good music, the galleries, and the new cinema.

The New York Times

The name of the game is still entertainment.

—Fat Bernie

Bernie G.—known to the trade as Fat Bernie the Gossip Broker, the best columns plugger in the business—starts each morning repeating the daily routine he has followed for the last nine years.

Next to his bed on a long wooden table he keeps his column items—Bernie's joys—stacked in orderly rows, typed three to a sheet:

> Judy Garland sobbing on the phone to me from Hollywood ("They fired me . . . why could they be so cruel to my children and me? G—damn them, it stinks!") was one of my saddest experiences as a reporter. Judy is at the end of her financial rope now. We were all moved.

Over the items are penciled dates and the names of gossip columnists. Above the Garland item: "Wilson June 7; Winch. June 8; Boyle June 10." So far no takers for Judy's despair.

Fat Bernie lifts himself out of bed, puts on his blue silk robe, sips his morning coffee, and begins to route his items. He examines each stack of what's gone where and who's seen what. Fat Bernie, who could never waste an item, sees that each reject gets another chance.

Fat Bernie is fat. At two hundred and twenty-five pounds and five feet six, he is so large that he waddles. He has a huge neck, with what's left of black hair curled down over the back and sides of his head.

If Fat Bernie Gersten did not exist, Damon Runyon would have invented him. There is only one faint incongruity in the *Guys and Dolls* routine, and that's Bernie's speech. Although he has a heavy New York accent (born in Newark, New Jersey), Bernie is educated (B.S., College of the City of New York) and sounds it.

Bernie has no regular clients, and he gets no retainers. He works on a strictly free-lance basis for the press agents and the public-relations firms that handle the big stars. They can't be bothered with the nuisance of daily gossip columnists; nonetheless they have clients who like to see their names in daily print.

Bernie receives a flat rate of eight dollars for a client's name mentioned in any of the New York gossip columns, except for Earl Wilson's, which has the largest syndication and for which Bernie gets ten dollars. Obviously, when Fat Bernie can "build a pyramid"—that is, cram two or three names into one item— he can make a lot of money.

While Cary Grant was making a film in New York, he stayed at a plush midtown hotel. Each morning for seven weeks the hotel barber would come to Grant's suite to give him a morning shave. Bernie gave the barber twenty a week to remember the star's morning remarks. Then Bernie sold the remarks to the columns for twenty dollars apiece.

Most major New York restaurants, as well as the stars, depend on public-relations firms to keep their names before the public. Most of the firms farm out their restaurants to Bernie along with the celebrities:

> Ethel Merman, resting from her chores as femme lead in the B'way smash *Hello, Dolly*, quipped to close friend Woody Allen at Max's Kansas City last night: "If you don't learn to write, nobody'll ever be able to read your picket sign."

That item, in Ed Sullivan's *New York Daily News* column, "Little Old New York," netted Fat Bernie twenty-eight dollars —twelve from the firm that represents Miss Merman and *Hello, Dolly* (Bernie charges four dollars for a Broadway play when mentioned with a star's name, or six for the show's title alone); eight covering Woody Allen, charged to his press agent; and the last eight from the office that represents Max.

The demise of the *World Journal Tribune* had its effect on

a great many New Yorkers. It most certainly affected Fat Bernie. Without the *Trib*, Bernie has only three major papers to
work with in Manhattan. "Of course, there's always the out-of-
town papers—Kup always takes stuff [*Chicago Sun-Times*' Irv
Kupcinet], but it's not the same—the whole thing is for the
benefit of the stars—and face it, your typical star just doesn't
give a damn about the *Sun*."

Bernie is also skeptical of magazines: "For one thing, they
don't break the stuff for two or three months, and it's impossible
to keep track of—I can't afford to tie up one item for two or
three months. If a piece doesn't hit, I've got to know right away
and reroute it."

Fat Bernie never knows where a news tip might come from,
so he tries to get along with everyone. It's vital for him to get
along with the columnists, and he prides himself on keeping
good working relationships with all of them. "They have to
both depend on me and ignore me—if they see me too much,
they might get nervous. That's why I have to keep up on their
working habits—like where Leonard Lyons is for lunch or where
Earl Wilson is in the afternoon. I keep all their schedules in
my head. Sometimes when one of their secretaries or their
wife can't find them, they call me. I always know." Dorothy
Kilgallen was the only columnist that ever gave Bernie trouble.
"I couldn't get along with that woman no matter what. She
used to send my items back to me with wisecracks in the margin.
Sometimes they were funnier than the items, but it always hurt.
I was very sorry when she passed away, but I'll tell you the
truth, I go out to the cemetery every now and then just to make
sure she's still there."

Bernie never throws anything out. Aside from the table
stacked with column notes, his apartment is literally filled with
stacks of old magazines and back issues of newspapers from all
over the country, as well as stacks of notes and theater pro-
grams.

After Bernie spends his hour or two routing items, he reads the day's papers. He first carefully reads each of the gossip columns: there are seven in the New York papers that he services regularly, and another nine for which he often claims bills. Bernie frequently identifies as many as ten items that he has planted in a single morning, which explains how he earns thirty thousand dollars a year.

Fat Bernie bases most but not all of his items on fact— "Most people don't believe most of what they read in the columns —they just like to read about stars, whether it's true or not." The columnists on whom Bernie depends for his livelihood are, however, more interested in facts. They frequently call a restaurant to find out if Tony Randall was indeed there on the previous evening eating the chef's *ottopode al forno*. The restaurants, however, have learned that if they deny the presence of a star they are quickly dropped from Fat Bernie's beat and from the columns.

Bernie feels that gossip columns serve a useful function. "They might not be the most important thing in the world, but millions of people read 'em daily, and it's our job to make them as interesting as possible. The role of the gossip columnist, the Broadway reporter, or whatever you want to call it, and the columns plugger, his duty and his importance, is to not bear false witness against his neighbor. There's got to be someone who tells it fairly and squarely, like it is. That's me, among the pluggers, and Earl and Leonard Lyons from the columnists."

After checking the columns, Bernie turns to his black accountant's book, in which he records the fruits of the previous day, then relaxes and leisurely reads the entire *Post* of the preceding evening and then glances through the *News*. He only bothers with the *Times*—no gossip columnists—on Sunday. Although he has not had particularly good luck with Lewis Funke's "News of the Rialto" (Broadway) or Abe Weiler's film notes in the Sunday *Times*, he keeps trying, and he does break items there occasionally. Bernie feels that the class of the *Times* is worth the effort.

After Bernie has routed his items, done his accounts, and read the papers, he rises up again and puts on a white-on-white shirt with collar points that droop almost to his waist, and selects a silk suit from a closet full of silk suits. Fat Bernie, who is oblivious to fashion, wears silk suits and white silk ties as regularly as silk suits and white silk ties go in and out of fashion. When he's dressed, Bernie is ready to begin his rounds, hunting for items.

He always carries a reporter's pad and an Old-Fashioned drinking glass in a black briefcase. The pad is to jot down what he calls "Gotham Gossip." The glass is to hold. Bernie spends his days in bars and restaurants, and finds that if he's not careful he's drunk by five in the afternoon and poorer the next day when doing his accounts. He eats at the Alamo Chile House on 44th Street and at Al's Tri-Rite Deli-Delite and Broadway Lunch near Times Square, but spends his working day in Sardi's, "21," Downey's, and the like. He has discovered that if he takes his glass out of his briefcase and holds it when he enters a restaurant, bartenders leave him alone and friendly customers do not insist that he have another drink.

During the years Fat Bernie has been a columns plugger, he has worked steadily, funneling news into the columns and occasionally planting an item in *Time* or *Life* or *Newsweek*. "Getting the stuff in *Life* impresses the stars. The agents like the columns, but for the stars it's all *Time* and *Life*."

Although Bernie prefers to work in New York—going from restaurant to restaurant, keeping his eye and ear attuned to the stars, meeting the press agents and courting the columnists, he occasionally works on out-of-town projects. One item that has become nearly a legend on Broadway is the result of Bernie's finagling. It also provides a glimpse into Bernie's sense of ethics about the creation of news.

When David Merrick was to open a county fair near Poland,

New York, Bernie bet Harvey Sabinson, Merrick's press agent, that he could turn the event into a column item. But Wilson, Lyons, and company, being none too enchanted with the notion of the Poland County Fair, turned the item down flat.

Bernie, upon investigation, learned of the existence of a small and obscure tribe of Shawnee Indians living outside Poland. Fat Bernie called the chief (whose name he cannot recall) and told him of Merrick's impending visit. Bernie suggested that the Shawnees make Merrick an honorary blood brother. Bernie promised the chief a great deal of publicity for the event, which he pointed out would be good for their souvenir business. The Shawnees not only delivered, but made Merrick *Brother Blwan-Blwan-Pum* (Collector of Wampum). The event made all the columns, with a headline in Lyons and Wilson—at twenty dollars per headline, which Sabinson personally matched, as the loser of the wager.

In general, if the event actually occurred, no matter what the circumstances, Fat Bernie does not consider any item the least shady: "It happened, didn't it? Just because I had the chutzpah to call that Indian doesn't mean it didn't really happen. It's not like I made it up."

On the other hand, Bernie is acutely aware of the dangers, both ethical and practical, in concocting items: "People are always suspicious, you got to be careful. The agents don't care, but if the stars read rigged plants they call the columns. It's crazy, they just cut their own throats, but that's the way it is."

Fat Bernie doesn't keep a real office. If he's not working out of his apartment or a restaurant or bar, he'll use the offices of the producers and press agents for whom he free-lances. The ad agency that handles most of Broadway's advertising keeps a special desk for him on opening nights. After any Broadway opening, the producer and the ad men gather in the agency's offices in the Sardi Building, to comb the advance copy of the reviews to make up the huge quote ads that fill the pages of the Sunday *New York Times'* "Arts and Leisure" section.

As they labor, Fat Bernie sits to one side, batting out column notes about the show. When he has completed three or four separate items (each a paragraph in length—although they are frequently cut to seven or eight words in the paper), he rips the sheet from the typewriter, careful to tear the bottom edge ("It's got to look hot—even if I wrote it yesterday, it's got to look hot"), and moves breathlessly downstairs into Sardi's main dining room, where he begins his hunt, a subtle thing.

As he enters Sardi's, he takes a casual look around the room, to spot Earl Wilson, Leonard Lyons, Hal Boyle, Jack O'Brian, Florabel Muir, Winchell, and the others. His prime target is Wilson, and if Wilson sees Bernie going first to O'Brian, Wilson will be upset. Bernie can't allow that; Wilson must get the first crack at the items. ("In the old days it used to be Winchell. Nobody reads Winchell any more, today it's all Wilson.")

If Wilson hesitates, Bernie has a choice. He can leave the item with him for a day to let him decide and thereby take it out of circulation but gain Wilson's favor (of vital importance), or he can demand that Wilson say yes or no on the spot, and, if it's no, move on to Lyons, Boyle, or Florabel. The problem is not to infuriate any of the writers by making them feel last on his list. This is no easy trick, when there are frequently three or four of them sitting within twenty-five feet of each other, and all acutely aware of Fat Bernie's presence. Bernie must operate diplomatically and table hop with agility.

In Sardi's they're used to him, so he doesn't have to pull out his Old-Fashioned glass.

Bernie stands at the door, waiting for Boyle to move away from Wilson so that he can make his first move. Boyle moves away and Bernie moves in. Wilson is sitting by the wall, watching a room full of stars and almost-stars.

"Earl, I see you for a moment?"

"Hi Bernie, whatta you got?"

"Exclusive to you. Warren Beatty's getting married. You want it?"

Fat Bernie pats his pocket as he speaks, indicating that the item—ripped and stuffed into an envelope—with more details is available; he's careful not to wave the envelope, conscious that at least one or two other writers are watching the conversation.

Wilson thinks for a moment, surveys the room, stirs his drink. "Who's Beatty marrying?"

"Don't know yet. Follow-up tomorrow, I hope."

Now Wilson thinks that Fat Bernie is trying to parlay the item into a number of placements—ten bucks for the first Beatty announcement, and another ten the next day when the woman's name is announced. Or maybe Bernie only represents Beatty for the moment and is trying to line up the girl's press agent before he places her name.

"I can use it Wednesday," Wilson finally says.

Bernie thinks for a moment; by Wednesday the item will be public information, no longer of value to him. Or maybe Wilson has another lead on the item. Bernie knows he's struck out with Wilson and prepares to move on to Lyons.

The problem now is that Bernie must move fast. He's given Wilson the lead on an item, and that means there's no longer an exclusive on it. Wilson could then break it after Bernie has given it as an exclusive to Lyons or Florabel.

He moves to Lyons.

"Len, got something for you."

"What?"

Lyons never looks at Bernie; he keeps his eyes trained on the crowd.

"Warren Beatty's getting married. You want it?"

"Who to?"

"Don't know."

"How long can I have it?"

"Tonight. It's hot."

"I don't think so, maybe Wednesday."

"I'll be back, I got more for later."

"Okay."

"See you, Len."

Fat Bernie moves away from Lyons with an eye out for Boyle. Boyle is already talking to one of the legmen from the office that represents Beatty.

News is out, Bernie has to work fast. He turns away from Boyle. *Don't be seen noticing . . . hang on to exclusive.* He moves toward the center of the crowd, working fast. *Find one . . . place it quick.*

Florabel Muir is roaming around.

Florabel'll do.

"Florabel, honey, I got to talk with you."

"You look like somebody's getting married."

Bernie smiles. "You want it?"

"Who else has it?"

"Nobody from me. Can you use it tomorrow?"

"Who is it?"

Fat Bernie hesitates, glances around the room, senses that he's about to lose the item, and moves in for the kill.

"Tomorrow, honey, yes or no?"

"Wonderful."

"Warren Beatty. An actress, in his next picture—name's still a see-key."

"Thanks, dear, maybe I'll use it."

Fat Bernie hands Florabel the envelope, a little crumbled from his pocket. Florabel floats away, and Fat Bernie spots Jack O'Brian heading his way. Bernie doesn't notice him, and ducks back to the elevator. He heads for Sardi's side door and out into the alley. A small note about the routing of the Warren Beatty piece in his notebook, and fat Bernie lurches toward the Stage Delicatessen and a pastrami sandwich.

When Fat Bernie was younger and in the big time, when his ambition was greater and before he began plugging the columns, he was a press agent for Zuckerman and Starr, touting Broadway shows and manufacturing the East Coast publicity for Paramount Pictures.

For a time, after the coming of television and the folding of Zuckerman and Starr, Fat Bernie ran his own office, but he was never able to adjust to the daily routines of cranking out press releases and supervising accounts payable; at the time, column notes bored him, and for a while he considered getting out of show business and going to work for the *Daily News*. In those days Bernie was a little thinner, had a little more hair, had not yet found his four-room rent-controlled apartment in the East 90s, and was a little less content. As an employee he earned less than a third of what he was later to make as an independent column plugger.

Although the early days of Bernard and Associates were financially shaky, it's a time Bernie recalls with some pleasure. "I used to take any kind of accounts that I could get. In those days I really had to hustle. I used to hang around places where I might be able to make a couple of bucks, or maybe meet somebody important. One of the places I hung around was the TV stations. I used to go backstage at all the amateur hours. Arthur Godfrey's Talent Scouts, Ted Mack's, all those. They were all live in those days and I knew all the doormen, so I could get in. I'd look over the talent, and if somebody looked good, a comic, or a singer, I'd try to sign him up—plug his name to the columns for a few bucks.

"A lot of good talent started that way, and if they make it to being a star, they remember you. Simple stuff, like 'So and so, lovely young thrush, made the fellas swoon and moon in her Ted Mack debut last night, big things for this blond-haired, blue-eyed cutie.' Stuff like that. That, in Wilson—gives the girl a thrill she'll never forget. And I make a few bucks, too. Word started getting around that I was making a specialty out of amateur shows, so the contestants would start getting in touch with me, asking me to take them on. I could usually pick the good ones. I had a rule: no baton-twirlers and no kids. That was me. I usually just took on the good bets, but sometimes I took a flyer on a long shot, you can never really know for sure who's going to make it to star.

"There was this one guy who talked me into plugging for him, I forget his name, but he was billed as the Dancing Chicken. He was from out West, and he came all the way to New York to get on Ted Mack and break into show business. He practically begged me to plug him to the columns. His life ambition was to be in Wilson. So I took him on. He was a nervous wreck before the show, but he said if he could get in Wilson he'd go through anything. When the show started, Ted Mack came out on stage and announced, 'And now, so-and-so, the Dancing Chicken!' Then the big gold curtain went up and there was this guy in a plaster-of-Paris chicken suit, about six feet high, with a big white belly and skinny wings that sort of flapped. His feet stuck out the bottom with little paper claws tied onto his dancing shoes. And he danced. He did routine stuff—shuffles, slides, time steps, that kind of thing. Except he did it in a plaster-of-Paris chicken costume, that was his gimmick. Well, he was going along pretty good, but then he tried some fancy splits and turns, got cocky, and he lost his balance and fell down. He was on his back, just rocking, and his little chicken feet were sticking up in the air and he was wiggling them, trying to get his balance back. Only the suit was so heavy that he couldn't. The band kept playing and he kept rocking and wiggling, trying to get up. Finally the curtain came down and Ted Mack went out on stage and said, 'Thank you, Dancing Chicken.'

"The guy was really upset. He begged me not to tell Wilson what happened, and he begged for another chance. So Ted Mack let him come back the next week to try again. So the next week Mack comes out and says, 'And now, back again for a second time, the Dancing Chicken!' And the curtain comes up, only this time he didn't have the chicken suit on. It was broken or something. This time he was wearing a real high stovepipe top hat that covered his whole head and face, and the brim was sort of resting on his shoulders. And he was bare-chested. He had eyes painted on his chest—around the nipples, with little eyebrows drawn over them—and he had a lipstick kewpie-doll mouth painted around his belly button. And he sang. He could roll his stomach so it looked like the song was coming out of the belly button. He sang 'Over the Rainbow.' The trouble was the top hat kind of muffled the song. Maybe you could do that if you were a ventriloquist, or if you had a really loud voice like an opera singer. But he didn't. That guy was no ventriloquist, I'll tell you that. I plugged him a little bit, but it never got in Wilson, or anything. What he should've tried, if he wanted to do the singing, was a Ventrilo, one of those little metal things you put in your mouth, and you can throw your voice. But he decided to go back to the Dancing Chicken instead. He went back out West I guess, he never did get in Wilson, he just disappeared."

As a young man on the rise, what Fat Bernie lusted for, what he did with relish and what kept him number-one man with Zuckerman and Starr, was his success with stunts and publicity hoaxes. As a specialist for a large office with a staff to cope with the problems of daily press releases and the ins and outs of bulk mail, Bernie was free, for a time, to concoct public events and whip up extravaganzas.

During his Zuckerman and Starr days, and for the first year of Bernard and Associates, Bernie was responsible for developing a number of classic Broadway and Hollywood publicity stunts, many of which are still used. It was Bernie who first capitalized on "Banned in Boston" by splashing it across a full-page ad in *The New York Times* for the Esther Williams film *Sea Nymph Goes to College.* Among Fat Bernie's best-known stunts were the celebrity kidnappings rampant in the late forties and the ersatz jewelry heists popular in the early fifties.

When he first went to work for Zuckerman and Starr, Fat Bernie was assigned to group sales. After he had been there for six months, "monkeying around with a lot of Hadassah ladies," he recalls, Bernie got the chance that led to his first great publicity coup. Zuckerman and Starr were handling the press for *Tiger Rag*, the musical based on the life of Benny Goodman.

The publicity was slanted toward the Goodman fans, with giveaways of his records and personal appearances. Each week a large portion of the publicity budget went for payola to keep Goodman's records on the radio. "Okay, except we weren't selling any groups for it. I asked Harry Starr if I could take a crack. He said, 'Sure, why not? Get the kid from the mail room, get the porter, get the cleaning woman, so everybody should take a crack.' "

Bernie felt that the highbrow approach—pushing the music—had done its job with the people who were interested, and it was time to move on. His solution is obvious to him now, but at the time he tried to think of stunts using rags. "I didn't want to blow it, it was a big chance, believe me—I had group sales up to here." Among Bernie's solutions, all of which were vetoed by Harry Starr, was: "Dress up some rag man in a tiger suit and put him in the show with his cart." That one was squelched by Irene Gordon, who produced and directed the show.

The solution that was Fat Bernie's ticket out of group sales and into the limelight came when Irene was about to post *Tiger Rag's* closing notice. "For a last-ditch try, Harry wanted to put a live tiger in the show—the second act was pretty dull anyway—but Irene said no. What we decided for the one last try was to put a tiger outside the theater before the matinee. Harry knew about this wild-animal farm with a tiger, so I shlepped up to Connecticut on the train to rent it. Way in the back of this wild-animal place, tied up to a tree, was the tiger. All it was doing was sleeping. I found out that's all it ever did. The damn thing must have been sixty years old. The wild-animal farm was run by a guy named Colaby, who said he was on a safari once in Africa. Colaby had a little shack out front where he sold tickets for the animals and dirty postcards. Colaby, who, besides never being on any safari farther than Waterbury, is also a crook who gets a hundred and seventy-five bucks plus expenses (which turn out to be another seventy-five bucks) for one afternoon for that tiger. Harry went along with it because there weren't any tigers for rent in New York and this was the only tame tiger in New England. The only trouble the thing gave us was getting it on and off Colaby's truck, which was also about sixty years old. It didn't want to get up, so Colaby had to give it a sedative which was about the size of a football. By the time we got it on the truck to go to New York, the damned thing was so drugged that it couldn't move even if it wanted to. Harry was supposed to come along and help, but he crapped out and I had to do it all myself.

"The tiger rumbled around a little on the West Side Highway. All that stopping and starting bothered him, I guess. But mostly he slept all the way. When we got into town Colaby pulled right in front of the theater—right on Broadway—before the matinee on Wednesday afternoon. I had three girls from the show in tiger-skin bikinis handing out flyers, so there was already a pretty big crowd. My part was to lead the tiger off the truck over to the girls, where Colaby is supposed to kick it, so it'll growl. Then I yell, '*Tiger Rag* tickets now on sale at the Winter Garden Theatre, don't miss this exciting show.' Then Colaby is supposed to kick him again, and he growls some more. After that, one of the girls is supposed to swoon or faint.

"You have to remember, I also have about six photographers there. Four of them we hired, the other two were from a photo tip that I sent the papers. One was from the *News*—they'll take a picture of anything—and the other was from the *Mirror*. Colaby backed the truck up on the curb and damn near ran over Harry

Starr, who was pretending to keep the girls organized. He had a bugle with him so there could be a fanfare when we got the tiger off the truck. He kept yelling, 'Get your ass in gear, sonny, get your ass in gear.' I crawled into the back with Colaby to get the tiger out, except the damn thing was still too doped up to move.

"When we got it out in the open, Harry got a glimpse of it and really got excited. He was still yelling, 'Get your ass in gear.' Then he began blowing the bugle. He was trying to play 'Sing Sing Sing,' which was from the show, and also from Benny's Carnegie Hall concert, but it kept coming out like 'Taps.' Well, with the bugle and all that sun and all those people out there, it was all too much for the tiger.

"He got about six steps down the ramp and he started growling and heaving and vomiting. The crowd went crazy. They started running and screaming. One thing about New York, the minute something's happening, there's a crowd right away. Some lady yells out, 'A lion, there's a lion,' and the chase is on. People start screaming and showing up from all over. The photographers are having a field day—they're shooting everything. I get so excited I forget to yell my line, and the girl who is supposed to swoon starts getting sick herself. Everybody is running around except the tiger, he's just laying there in the sun in his vomit, moaning. Colaby is yelling, 'Give him air, the cat needs air.' Harry was blowing the bugle and steering the photographers over to the marquee, so the pictures would have the name of the show in them. He loved it.

"With the excitement of the whole thing, I got pretty carried away. The crowd got bigger, I kept spieling, the photographers kept shooting, and the tiger just kept lying in the sun at Fifty-first and Broadway, slithering around in the mess. Some cops showed up and made us break it up. There must have been five hundred people there by then. The crowd was backed up almost to Fifty-second Street, and traffic was stopped on Broadway. We got the tiger back in the truck, we just picked it up—

it took both of us and a cop to do it—and Colaby took him back to Connecticut.

"I thought it might break in the *News* or something. But I never saw anything like it—all the papers, radio, *Time*, *Life*, *Newsweek*, and all the wires—the whole schmeer. All the headlines were about an escaped tiger ruining a performance of *Tiger Rag*. It was even in the *Paris Tribune*. The *News* said, 'Rabid Beast Unleashed in Midst of Broadway Crowd.' Most of the heads though were about a 'Wild Tiger on Broadway.' They all thought the tiger was part of the show, which was fine with me. Anyway, tickets picked up right away and the show ran for another six months. Harry took most of the credit, but I never had to go back to group sales again.

"I heard a couple years ago where the tiger died. I sent it to Lyons for free, but he didn't use it. Oh yeah, his name was Rajah."

"There was this Milton who used to hustle around a lot. He did some leg work for me—I'd give him a couple of dollars and he'd run around. He said he wanted to learn column plugging, but that was just to butter me up. What he really wanted was to get his own name in the columns, plus he made up items all the time—that's two things that are death for a columns plugger. Before I gave him the job of legman, he used to follow me around, pushing one thing or another, always promoting.

"Milton had some good ideas, but he had trouble putting them across. He didn't make too good of an impression on people till you got to know him. For one thing, he talked through his nose and he thought he was a really sharp dresser. When I first met him, he always had a hanky sticking out of his pocket and it was embroidered in red across the top: 'Care to Dance?' That's how sharp this Milton was. But I have to admit he did have some good ideas. Back around fifty-six or fifty-seven, Milton had this idea for the airlines, to start vaudeville shows on flights. He was going to line up singing stewardesses and baggage guys who could tap dance and pilots that could do jokes. Not while they were actually flying the planes, but maybe the co-pilot. The copilot just sits there most of the time anyway. He could do a few jokes without any trouble, if you got the right man and the right material. It was going to spin off into a big vaudeville revival—he was going to put it on buses and trains, too—on every mode of modern transportation, and Milton was going to get in on the ground floor. My part was plugging it. He was set and moving with TWA and then the airlines decided to go with movies and Milton's idea was scratched. Just dumped on the spot. He was very depressed over that for a long time, but he bounced back. He had a lot of ideas, Milton. Elevators with Muzak are really just spin-off from Milton's idea, but he never got a cent. He was a visionary.

"One time Milton heard about this new film process—you could change the color of something after the film was made. If something was red, you could make it blue. If it was a cloudy day, you could make it sunny. It was some invention. He heard about this Italian producer who didn't like the color of the grass in a picture he was making, so he painted it. This Italian guy actually painted all the grass. And the topper is he painted it green. If you're going to do that you should at least come up with another color. But this Italian just did it another shade of green. Cost a fortune. Milton figured with this invention you wouldn't have to do that. You could shoot any grass, anywhere, and then fix it up to the color you want in the lab.

" 'Bernie,' he said to me in the Alamo Chile House, where we used to meet for lunch a couple times a week, 'this thing is okay for features—changing grass and stuff—but that's small change. The action for this, the real dough, is tied into the now market, with a contemporary slant.' 'Okay,' I said. Milton said, 'The agencies need commercials with black actors in 'em. Am I right?'

"I knew something was up when he said "black actors," because Milton has called Negroes "Schwartzes" or at best "colored" all his life. All of a sudden he goes NAACP in the middle of the Alamo Chile House, but he was still talking through his same nose, and I knew it was some stunt and he was the same Milton.

" 'For the now market, they have to shoot the commercials all over again with black actors. Costs maybe forty or fifty thousand bucks apiece. My idea is this: we take every beer, toothpaste, soapsud, and deodorant spot we can get our hands on, run 'em through the invention, and turn all the white guys and gals black.'

"Milton figured he could make a hundred thousand a year as middle man on the deal. He had the sales and promotional rights tied up—purely on spec, but he had the rights. He wanted me to plug the thing to the columns to get it off the ground. And, knowing Milton, also get his name in the columns a whole lot. He wanted to make a demo film to give the agencies a graphic illustration of the invention's versatility. He wanted the demo to star Earl Wilson. The plan was to shoot Earl in his regular color and then reprocess him into a Negro, or as Milton was now saying all the time, 'a black actor.' With Earl being an uncontestable white, the agencies would see a dramatic example of what Milton was talking about, and with Earl starring he'd show that this was a strictly class operation. Also, he'd probably get his own name into the columns. My job was to sell Earl on it. That was my mistake. I gave Earl a rundown on the whole thing—softpedaling Milton's part in it, and pushing the racial-harmony end of it, because I know Earl's big on that. You don't see him picketing, but he's always going on telethons, so I figured that's the angle. I got to him over at '21,' where he was interviewing some actor. Now Earl has turned me down on a lot of stuff over the years—that's the way it goes. He takes some, rejects some. No big deal. But on this thing Earl got very upset. I mean he was mad. He called me and Milton racists and he was going to ban me from the column and everything. He didn't want to hear about the invention or about Milton again. He didn't even introduce me to the actor he was interviewing, which is very unusual, he's a very polite guy, Earl. The whole thing never took off without Earl. I got out when Earl did. If he wouldn't touch it, that was good enough for me."

"One time Milton asked me to plug a kid singer he was personal-managing. I floated a couple of items around—sold a single to Florabel and had a couple of small scores with Winchell, but nothing big. It meant a lot to Milton because when Winchell was really going he was the king, and a guy like Milton would fall all over himself for a mention. Winchell was so big that they made a picture out of his life, but he hated it. We had to pretend we didn't know anything about it. Winchell had guys watching the theater, and if any column plugger came in or out, Walter would ban him from the column. He had a lot of power until he started fading. When it was over for him it seemed like he had a power that didn't really exist. That was in the fifties. In the fifties Winchell was the one. At least for columns pluggers and press agents. With a guy like Milton, if Winchell would say 'Jump,' Milton would say, 'How high?' After I sent out the stuff about the kid singer, and I met him once, what Milton wanted was for me to introduce the kid to Earl. So I set it up.

"We were supposed to meet first, and I almost tripped over the kid. He was sitting in front of the Broadway Theatre, where Earl used to have his office. At first I thought the kid was just looking up miniskirts, which he was. This is a lunch I set up, not some little handshake and nice-to-see-you. Earl doesn't exactly go running off to lunch with every punk kid and his manager who wants to be a star. The kid's sitting on the sidewalk with his legs sticking straight out. Plus he's got an earring in one of his ears. A little gold one. He's supposed to meet Earl in ten minutes to go to lunch and he's sitting on the sidewalk with an earring, not to mention about six pounds of hair. Milton is standing there looking panicked. He's bent over the kid, shaking him by the shirt, yelling, 'Come on, damn it . . . come on.' No matter how much Milton shakes him, all the kid does is go 'Ummmph-mmmph,' with his mouth shut up tight. The more Milton shakes,

the more the kid goes 'Mmmmph.' It's like they're playing cha-
rades and Milton is losing.

" 'Bernie'—Milton gets up from the kid and takes me aside.
'Don't tell Earl.'

" 'What?'

" 'The kid can't talk.'

"Now I know that is not true—I heard him two days ago in
the Alamo—but I do know that whatever's going on, I'm not
taking him up to meet Earl with that earring on.

" 'I mean he can talk, but he won't. Not any more,' Milton
says to me.

" 'Why not?' Which seemed like a reasonable question.

" 'He says he can't talk any more because words are dead.'
Milton is hanging on to my coat and the kid is still sitting there.
He looks up at me and pretends to turn a little key in his mouth,
like a lock, and then he throws the key away. A regular Marcel
Marceau. 'He says from now on everything's film and words are
dead.'

" 'Pictures? He can't even break out as a singer,' I remind
Milton.

" 'That's what he said.' He decides this, according to Milton,
while he's sitting in front of the Broadway Theatre waiting to
go to lunch with Earl Wilson which will result in the only break
he's ever going to get. Then Milton starts this song and dance
about making the 'words are dead' stuff into an item. Earl is
really going to go for that. Milton says the last thing the kid
said before he stopped talking was 'Earl Wilson is the enemy of
language.' Now Earl, who never makes an enemy—that's the
beauty of him—is nothing but language. If he isn't language,
what is he? Pure words are all you get from him. But Milton
says that's what the kid said, and then he shut up. Milton said it
could make an item. Milton, who is about three feet tall and talks
through his nose, is going to tell me and Earl Wilson what is and
isn't going to make an item. He says, talking through his nose
and jumping around, 'It'll make a sen-sa-shun-al item for Earl.

It's a case of the real thing. For the now kids it's all over with words. He's where it's at.' By now Milton is really getting excited. He's pounding on the kid's head and starting to sweat. 'Bernie, see it: *"So-and-so, pop sensation, stops talking because words are dead!"* It'll be absafuckinlutely sen-sa-shun-al.' Now he's writing items for me, which he's about as good at as he is at personal-managing. That item, 'So-and-so, pop sensation . . .'? That's an amateur item right in front. It's got no rhythm, no style, no grab, and it's lousy. An item like that's very tricky to handle, it's got to be very sharp to work. It's got to jump off the page and grab you. It's got to sing and make you hum along or it's nowhere. Like Milton and his kid singer. Milton grabs the kid's shirt and starts shaking him. 'Say something, damn it. Say something.' The kid just said 'Ummmph-mmmph' again and sat there (that's when I caught him looking up the miniskirts). I thought Milton was going to cry, he was so upset. He kept saying, 'The kid's sen-sa-shun-al, it's sen-sa-shun-al.'

"I excused myself and went upstairs to tell Earl that the lunch was off, that the kid had laryngitis. I apologized and said we'd get together soon. Earl said okay, he wasn't hungry anyway."

Coppleman called Fat Bernie on a Friday morning at a quarter of eight to complain about the Dustin Hoffman item in Earl Wilson's Thursday column:

> Gotham's newest rider on a superstar-ship, Dustin (*The Graduate, Little Big Man*) Hoffman, has refused two major H'wood offers to work in NYC—seems Dusty can't leave his analyst long enough to go to sunland.

Bernie had placed that item with Wilson the week before, and when it hadn't appeared by Wednesday he figured it was dead. The call from Coppleman, the analyst in question, and the early hour caught him off balance.

"You will forgive the hour, sir. However, this is my only free time."

"It's okay!"

"I am calling in reference to the column of Mr. Earl Wilson in the *New York Post* of yesterday afternoon."

"What item?"

"Regarding Mr. Dustin Hoffman."

"Oh, yeah."

"I as well as my colleagues consider it highly unethical, not to mention irresponsible, to make information of such a highly intimate and confidential nature public."

"Why you calling me?"

"Mr. Wilson tells me you are his agent in such matters. Information about a patient's psychic state is extremely confidential, as well as potentially volatile."

"You called Wilson?"

"Yes."

"This morning already?"

"Yes. His anxiety level is already dangerously high"— Fat Bernie lets out a slow whistle and considers Earl Wilson, who never gets up before eleven, being awakened at seven-thirty —"not to mention an acute distress. I would like to know, sir, how you are privy to such information?"

"Was he mad?"

"I think a more accurate description might be acutely distressed."

"Did he say anything about me?"

"I don't believe he is aware you were involved in this matter. I learned of your—"

"Wilson?"

"No, no. I am referring to Mr. Hoffman. I would not presume to offer a diagnosis of Mr. Wilson's anxiety level without an initial interview at the very least."

"Yeah, but when you woke him up—Wilson—was he mad? Acutely distressed or anything?"

"It was difficult to tell. I'm not certain that I did wake him. But, more to the point—"

"If you called him already this morning you woke him. And he was mad."

"Be that as it may, the point is, I need to know your sources."

"You mean about Hoffman?"

"Yes."

"I don't know. I guess I heard it around."

"I would like to point out to you, sir, that the nature of a doctor-patient relationship is extremely confidential, not to mention delicate."

"Well, he's gotta learn how to get along with the press if he's gonna be a star."

"Bandying about half-truths regarding that relationship is dangerous to both patient and doctor."

"The press's first obligation is to the truth."

"And I suspect its second obligation is to sensationalism. We will, however, overlook the entire incident if you can assure me you'll declare a moratorium on news concerning my patient's psychic state. I hope Mr. Hoffman's attorney will be as forgiving."

"Well, news is news, but we don't want to hurt anybody's feelings, so I guess it wouldn't hurt if I check with you for a medical opinion before we run anything on Hoffman. How's that?"

"Excellent. Now if you'll excuse me, my first patient is due."

"Who's that?"

"I beg your pardon?"

"The first patient?" Bernie reaches over to the table next to his bed and gropes for his notebook. "I wondered if it was anybody in show business?"

"My work is extremely confidential."

"Do you have any other stars for clients?"

"As a matter of fact, several of my patients are from the

entertainment world. As you may know, the theater creates a great many pressures—"

"You handle Tennessee Williams?"

"My clients, I mean patients, are primarily performers."

"What's your first name, Doctor?"

"Alois. However, I fail—"

"That's A-l-?"

"A-l-o-i-s."

"How do you spell your last name?"

"C-o-p-p-l-e-m-a-n."

"What about Sammy Davis? You handle him? Zero Mostel? Who else besides Hoffman?"

"That's none of your business."

"But if I know, then I can check all the time with you, so we don't have this problem again."

"Please, I must get back to my work."

"How much do you charge?"

"That is confidential information."

"More than seventy-five an hour? Just say yes or no."

"Yes. No. My first patient is arriving. Good-by."

"Davis or Mostel?"

Dr. Coppleman hung up, and Fat Bernie sank back into bed, smoothing his red size-48-short Sulka pajamas, and waited for an angry call from Wilson. As he dozed he phrased Coppleman items in his mind:

What famous young actor has his analyst begging the Press to lay off? The Doc sez, "It's rough on my boy, so come on, fellas, take it easy."

Or, he might kick it off with the Doctor:

Dr. Alois Coppleman, the $75-an-hour-plus shrink to the stars (Dustin Hoffman, etc.), has asked for a let-up on reports of the mental state of one of our town's most famous.

At nine o'clock Bernie decided Wilson wasn't going to call and chew him out after all, which meant Wilson was *really* angry. When he was upset he would call and yell for a few minutes to get it out of his system. Over the years, Bernie has learned how much contriteness soothes each columnist. For Wilson you sounded scared for a while and then pretty soon everybody is friends again, business as usual. But when he doesn't call to yell, that's when he's really upset. He just disappears—out when you call and busy if you can find him.

Bernie, upset from being awakened early by bad news, dawdled over his Danish at Al's Broadway Lunch and brooded about an angry Earl Wilson.

Friday mornings Bernie goes to the *New York Times* building on 43rd Street for an advance copy of Sunday's theater section, which is printed Wednesday night. Today, because he's lingered at Al's, he's behind schedule and doesn't get to the *Times* till after eleven. He mumbles hello to Sid Kone, the circulation man, who gives him the last advance copy of the paper. On the way out he picks up a copy of the three-star edition of the *Daily News* and walks back to Al's for a second breakfast.

He sits in the back again with another coffee and Danish, glancing through the *News* entertainment section. Pushing the *News* aside, he leafs through the *Times*, scanning the "News of the Rialto" and "Film Notes," the closest thing to gossip in the *Times*:

> After seeing just two pages of an outline Twentieth Century–Fox has snatched the screen rights to *Answered Prayers*, Truman Capote's novel-in-progress, for a down payment of $350,000. The full price could go as high as $750,000, depending on sales of the book.

Bernie chews his Danish and stares at the item, turning its phrases around in his mind. "*Answered Prayers*. More Capote."

It was Fat Bernie who first broke the news of the film sale of *In Cold Blood*. The publicity office at Twentieth still sends him a check for twenty-five dollars every time the title appears in the columns. *Answered Prayers*, however, is news to Bernie, which means the *Times* has a real exclusive.

He reads it again and considers: *Times won't be on the stand till Saturday night. . . . Wilson closes his Saturday column at one-thirty this afternoon.* Now Fat Bernie prides himself on always getting his own items. He has worked hard over the years building a network of informants: the bartenders, head-waiters, and production secretaries who keep him posted on the comings and goings of the stars. Bernie has spent ten years carefully establishing good will with the press agents and columnists who keep him in gossip and in business. His financial success rests on his reputation—for, if Bernie sometimes exag-gerates an item or makes one up, he is known in the trade for never double-planting—giving the same item to two columnists at once. Feeding the Capote item to Wilson from an advance copy of the *Times* is unethical, but the chances are it'll never be traced to Bernie anyway, and if the maneuver impresses Wilson enough to smooth over the Hoffman incident, Bernie feels it's worth the chance. With luck, the *Times* will be angry that Wilson beat them to the Capote item, but will never know how it happened.

Bernie looks up at the clock—eleven-thirty—gets up quickly, and takes Al's portable typewriter from behind the counter, pulls Friday's menu out of it, and carries it back to his table. He shoves a piece of Manila copy paper from his briefcase into the carriage and punches out:

THE MIDNIGHT EARL

Dept. of hard work: 20th Cent. Fox just paid Truman (IN COLD BLOOD) Capote $350,000 for a 2-page outline of his next book, ANSWERED PRAYERS. When the tome is finished Truman could get as much as $750,000. You heard it here first.

Fat Bernie tears the paper out of the typewriter so that the news will look as hot as it is. If he can get it to Wilson before one-thirty, Wilson can break it before the *Times* is on the stands and Bernie will be back in Wilson's good graces. First, though, he has to find Wilson. Fat Bernie has studied Earl Wilson's working habits for years. In the afternoons Wilson can usually be found at Gallagher's or Downey's, and after the theater he'll probably show up at Sardi's. Bernie knows that when Wilson is awakened early, as he was by the Coppleman call, he is likely to stop at Downey's for brunch. Bernie fishes a handful of dimes out of the envelope of dimes he keeps in his briefcase and moves into Al's phone booth, taking his coffee and the remnants of a second Danish with him.

The afternoon man at Downey's is Tony della Rocca, and he and Bernie have been trading favors for years.

"Tony?"

"Yeah?"

"Bernie. Earl Wilson there?"

"No, but I got Leslie Caron."

"Caron, huh?" Bernie cradles the phone between his shoulder and the folds of his size-twenty neck and makes a note in his book: *Leslie Caron on a rare Gotham visit, dropped in at Jim Downey's Steak House for an early afternoon refueling . . .*

"Yeah, she just walked in. She's got one of them big hats on, I can't see her face." Tony pauses for a moment and then almost as an afterthought adds, "She's by herself, too."

. . . playing Greta ("I vant to be alone") Garbo in a floppy . . . "What color's the hat?"

"Too dark to tell."

. . . gray hat. "Thanks, Tony."

"You comin' over?"

"No, I gotta find Wilson." Bernie leaves the phone-booth door open while he tries to concentrate on Wilson's irregular morning schedule. His bulk fills the booth and the glass door starts to steam. As Bernie squirms on the stool he feels his huge bottom ooze over the sides of the seat. He wipes his forehead with his hand and mops a pudgy palm across his shiny sharkskin pants. Al brings him more coffee. Fat Bernie sips, and on the chance that Wilson has been trying to get him calls his answering service and learns that, although Wilson hasn't been heard from, Coppleman has called twice, at nine-fifty-five and again at ten-fifty-five. Bernie glances up at the clock: eleven-thirty. He stuffs another dime in and calls Coppleman.

"Ah, Bernard, how are you?"

"Okay."

"I wanted you to know that I've spoken with Mr. Hoffman's attorneys. I've suggested that a lawsuit at this time might complicate things, medically speaking."

"Okay."

"I hope that will make matters a little easier for you."

"It'll help."

"Good."

"Did you talk to Wilson again, Doctor?"

"No, no, I haven't. Do you think he'll still be upset?"

"I guess so."

"But you'll still be supplying him with news?"

"I guess so."

"Good."

Bernie shifts around in the phone booth again, uncomfortable talking to Coppleman and anxious to resume his search for Wilson. "Dr. Coppleman, is there something else we need to talk about, because if not—"

"As a matter of fact, now that you ask, there is something. . . ."

"What?"

"Ahh, well, it might be advantageous to me personally to have a little something in the papers about my wife's birthday."

"Mmm."

"I rarely read the columns myself, of course, but it would mean a lot to her. You see, at the moment our relationship is a bit strained, and this might—"

"In Wilson?"

"Actually, Leonard Lyons is more what I had in mind. Do you think you can arrange it?"

"I'll see what I can do."

"I'd appreciate that. Her birthday is on the twenty-first. It's Cynthia. Cynthia Coppleman. Thank you."

"Sure. Maybe you could do me a favor."

"I'll try, Bernard."

"You could keep me posted on some of your clients—"

"I don't understand—"

"It wouldn't have to look like it necessarily came from you."

"I couldn't give out any information that might prove damaging—"

"No, no. Nothing damaging."

"Well, as long as it wasn't damaging."

"No, no. For instance, I heard Hoffman's going to do a film for Sidney Lumet. Is that true?"

"It'll never happen."

"Lumet make the offer?"

"Oh, yeah, but he'll turn it down, take my word. He may do a few TV guest shots, but that's all for a while."

"What about Mostel?"

"I don't handle him, but I hear he's not going to work for a few months."

"Mmm."

"Anything else?"

"Not at the moment, thanks."

"However, ahh . . . Well, Bernard, there is one thing more."

"Yeah?"

"If you should ever feel the need—that is, I'm sure your work must be very exacting, and if you think it could be of any value, I'd be glad to try to find an hour or two to meet with you each week."

"Yeah?"

"I'm heavily booked, of course, from eight to six daily, in fact, but if you feel it would be of value to you, I think I can clear the time."

"I dunno, your rates are kinda steep."

"I'm certain we could work something out. We are talking, of course, of therapy, which is far less expensive than analysis—"

"Therapy, huh?"

"There are frequently things I would like printed in the papers."

"You shrink me and I plug items for you?"

"Something like that could be arranged."

"I'd have to think about that."

"Good, good."

"I'm kinda rushed right now, but I'll let you know."

Bernie hangs up, makes a few more jottings about Cynthia Coppleman's birthday. Al brings him more coffee. "What time is it?" Al points to the Pepsi-Cola clock above the cash register and wanders back to the counter. Eleven-forty-five. Bernie slurps his coffee and stuffs another dime in the phone. On an off chance that they'll know, he calls Wilson's office. Three rings and no answer, which means that the answering service will pick up. Bernie curses Wilson and his answering service, which usually has three-day-old information.

"I'm looking for Earl."

"Who's calling?"

"I'm looking for Earl."

"Leave your name and number, I'll have him call you."

"Do you know where he is?"

"May I have a number where he can reach you?"

"I'll be out. It's important. Do you—"

"Mr. Wilson's having breakfast."

Bernie thinks for a moment. Wilson sometimes stops off for poached eggs at the Stage Delicatessen. "Is he at the Stage Deli—"

"I don't know, sir—"

Bernie cuts her off, presses a fourth dime into the phone, and calls Jack Luft, the cash-register man at the Stage.

"Yeah, he's here. He just got his eggs. Should I tell him to wait?"

"No, no. Don't tell him I called. I'm coming over; only Jack, don't let him leave." Bernie gulps the last of his coffee, squeezes out of the phone booth, and slaps a dollar on the register. Outside he grabs a cab and heads toward 54th Street. In the back of the cab Bernie stares nervously at the Capote note. He folds it into a small white envelope and, using his briefcase for a desk, writes with a green Pentel across the front of the envelope: MR. EARL WILSON. *Private.* As they near the Stage, Bernie notices the driver's clock. *A little past noon . . . if Wilson's alone . . . it's all okay.* Bernie gets out and hands the driver a buck. "I'll walk from here." Lugging his briefcase and starting to sweat, Bernie moves quickly toward the deli. He plows through the double glass doors and searches for Wilson. Jack looks up, nods, and points toward the back. *Wilson.* Fat Bernie stops abruptly and modulates from nervousness into a more casual key. *Take it easy . . . smooth, like Earl.* Wilson is by himself facing the front, mopping up the remains of his poached eggs with a corner of rye toast. He sees Bernie and the trace of a flush appears at his throat, just above his tie. He looks back at his plate as Bernie saunters over.

"Earl baby, how are you?"

Wilson looks up at Bernie, doesn't answer, gives a little shrug, and finishes off a large glass of orange juice.

"Guess you got a phone call this morning, huh Earl?"

"I guess we both did."

"Yeah, well don't worry about it. They can't touch you. That item was a hundred per cent true, and I heard from the lawyers—no problem."

Wilson signals for more coffee.

"It's good I ran into you, Earl. Mind if I sit down?"

Wilson shrugs again, noncommittally. Bernie pulls out one

of the chrome and red leatherette chairs and calls to the counter, "Gimme coffee black and a Danish." As Bernie sits he casually puts his hand in his jacket pocket, as if there were a gun there.

"Whatta you got?"

Bernie takes his time. *Let him get interested.*

"Look, if you got something for me, just give it to me, and cut the games. I already had enough tricks for one day."

Bernie droops his head and looks contrite. *Nervous . . . look nervous.* He shifts his weight on the chair. The waitress delivers his order. Bernie draws the slightly crumpled envelope from his pocket and hands it to Wilson, like an olive branch. Wilson accepts and tears it open as Bernie takes a large bite of Danish, up to the prune center. Wilson reads.

"Capote again?"

"Absolute exclusive."

"How long?"

"Through tomorrow, then it breaks big. Real big."

"Lyons doesn't have it?"

Bernie looks hurt. "Absolute exclusive."

Wilson grunts, gets up, and heads for the phone. Halfway to the booth he stops abruptly and turns back to Bernie. Before he can say anything Bernie flips him a dime. Wilson grins and goes to the phone. Bernie watches him dial and takes another bite of Danish. The remains of the prune squeeze between his teeth and the icing stains the corners of his mouth. With Wilson in the phone booth filing the Capote story, Fat Bernie eases away from the table. He goes by the register, waves to Jack, making a circle with his thumb and forefinger, and smiles back toward the phone booth. Then Fat Bernie wanders back across town to the Luxor Baths, where he'll read the Sunday *Times*, write up the Caron item for Leonard Lyons, and think about Coppleman's offer as he sits and soaks in the steam. ●

309.1
Freeman, David
U. S. Grant in the city.

WITHDRAWN

WITHDRAWN

8-72